WE CAN STILL HEAR THEM CLAPPING

BY MARCIA KEEGAN

NORTHTOWN-SHILOH

FLARE BOOKS/PUBLISHED BY AVON

To Norm and my vaudevillian friends
who helped me compose this book.

WE CAN STILL HEAR THEM CLAPPING is an
original publication of Avon Books. Published in a
Flare edition, this work has never before appeared
in book form.

AVON BOOKS
A division of
The Hearst Corporation
959 Eighth Avenue
New York, New York 10019

The golden age of vaudeville reached its heights in the first quarter of the twentieth century. During this period, its popularity and its impact spread throughout the nation. But its home, its heart and its source of nourishment never left a few square blocks surrounding Times Square and Broadway in New York City.

Vaudeville spawned a host of artists who gained greater glory in other entertainment mediums and in other entertainment centers, but also gave birth to a much larger number of artists who never quite made it to the top. Many of them never left those few square blocks that were the center of their art, and a host of them live there still, in old and deteriorating hotels that are remnants of their once exciting and glamorous world.

In 1967, when the headlines of New York City newspapers announced the start of demolition of a number of these hotels, I was commissioned by the Office of Economic Opportunity for a day to do a brief photographic essay on the reaction of the residents who would be affected by the demolition. What started as a simple assignment turned out to be a sustained and still consuming involvement. All the vaudevillians appearing in this book, as well as many others, have become an important part of my life. They have touched me in countless ways. Their talents were celebrated before I was born, but the spirit and the spark which they must have had at the peaks of their careers remain very much within them. They were entertainers then, and are entertainers now.

Morris Lloyd, at age 86, performs as a clown in hospitals and senior citizen homes; Phil Foote organized his own band and performs at the New York Jazz Museum; Lillian Ashton and Edna Thayer are working on a musical comedy in which they hope to appear on Broadway; Al Greiner teaches piano and performs weekly in a New York City restaurant; Sally Demay and Eleanor Gould are busy making television commercials; and, Strawberry Russell tap dances and plays his guitar with the same zest of fifty years ago.

The ties to Broadway which all of them share go beyond their physical presence and go beyond their memorable pasts. These vaudevillians are still "playing Broadway" and they are playing it the only way they know how—with pride, with sincerity and with everything they've got. Only the audience has been diminished.

These are entertainers who are happiest when they are giving of themselves. And, so long as they feel that what they are giving is wanted and enjoyed, they will maintain their dignity no matter what their physical circumstances may be. They were pleased and eager to tell their stories and to share with others their memories and hopes. They had a lot to tell and this book is their story —the way they told it.

Marcia Keegan

RAE DAVIS

I came to New York from New Haven when I was 17 and when I got to Grand Central, I said to a cop — I want to go to the center of New York. He said, which center? I said I'm going into show business, so he sent me to 47th Street and I found a hotel there. I've never lived anywhere else except Times Square.

I got a job in a chorus and once you're in, you're in. I did vaudeville, burlesque, musical comedy. Once I was in a physical-culture act at the Palace. That was with a man who called himself Hyatt the Superman. I was the announcer. He used to stand outside the Palace holding four horses, showing how strong he was.

I traveled a lot. The only thing I didn't play was circus.

I love Broadway at night. It hasn't changed much since I retired. There's just more of everything.

"Queen Elizabeth"

LILLIAN ASHTON

I'm Lillian Ashton. I'm 82 years old and I've been in vaudeville all my life. I was booked from England as an entertainer on the William Morris tour in 1911. I played in shows all over in peak vaudeville and low vaudeville. I entertained all the soldiers and sailors. I also shook hands with the late President Roosevelt.

My mother and father were both in show business. My brother was a ventriloquist and he invented the first walking doll.

How I came to America is a long, sad story. You see, I was married when I was 14 years old, and about a year later I had a little girl, Florence. Later, I was working in London in a lot of shows. Because I was away so long, my husband took up with another woman and they had my little girl. So one day, because I had a millionaire's son who liked me and also because I was doing well on my own, I decided to get my daughter, who was with her father in Newcastle.

I went with a friend who had been my midwife and had brought Flo into this world. My daughter and two little girls, who belonged to the other woman, were on the beach and I saw her and went to kidnap her. I told her I was her mother and we got in a cab and we took her to my friend's place. We put clean clothes on her and the next day we went to the court-house. Then I went to see my husband, who was staying with my parents, and the other woman started to fight with me. But I was strong. She wanted to disfigure me for life with a hatpin but I fought her, and my father, God bless him, finally got the hatpin out of her hand. So then I promised my husband I would send for him if he got away from that woman. But she threw vitriol in his face and he died from it.

I had two detectives escort me on the train to London and that woman was put in jail. She had two children and while she had my daughter, she had made my little girl go out and beg in the streets. She was only four years old at the time. I got my daughter back when she was about five, and we cleaned her up. I had a nurse and maid with me to take care of her because I was doing good and making good money. The millionaire's son liked me, but his father was against it and paid me a lot of money to stay away from his son. Actually, I didn't like the son very much, anyway.

In 1911, I came to America with my little girl because I was booked on the William Morris tour over here on the Keith's Fifth Avenue. Then I married another drunk. He was an American drummer playing with the Great Lafayette in England. I paid his fare over here, and he was to follow me later. Unfortunately, I always fell in love with the wrong kind of men. I bought a house in Newport, Rhode Island, and my second husband drank every night and, little by little, he took all my money. So I put my daughter in a convent school and I went on the road. It's a sad story. That was an awful time I went through. I had a lot of men after me, then and later, but I couldn't marry them if I didn't love them. Sometimes I'd make believe I would, but I couldn't, you know.

My parents died in 1917 in a bombing during the war in London, my mother with her makeup on. Very sad. I was over here when I got the cable. When my daughter got married in 1924, I went over to England and worked with a straight man for a year and a half. Then I came back.

In 1917, I was the one who introduced the song — "It's a Long Way to Tipperary" — sitting on a table in the old Putnam Building here, where the off-track betting place is now. I didn't write the song, but I was the first to sing it in America.

I also worked with Edna Thayer's parents in vaudeville and I've known Edna since she was three years old. We're still good friends, and I visit her often at the Automat to hear her sing.

Some of the jokes we did in vaudeville went like this: What's the best way to stop a horse from foaming at the mouth? Teach him how to spit. Guess who's the mother of Santa Claus? Merry Christmas!

I played in vaudeville with Sir Harry Lauder, Orson Welles, Ken Murray, Archie Leach. You know who Archie Leach is, don't you? Cary Grant. Charlie Chaplin and I were kids together in England. We played together in shows, pantomime.

I've been in some very big shows. *The Girl Behind the Counter, Very Good, Eddie,* to mention two. I was in Sir Harry Lauder's shows all over the old country. I was also the first woman to play with a big hat. I did a comedy act in vaudeville, which would open up with me in a wedding dress. Then I'd come back with an old shawl and bonnet singing, "Anybody Looking for a Widow." Then I'd come back with a big hat with 9,000 feathers on it and sing, "All for the Love of Mike." Now I'm all dressed up real nice this time, and I come out and tell the audience about the different petticoats I've received. It was a striptease.

I've a little pink petty from Peter.
And a little blue petty from John.
One green and yellow from some other
    fellow

September 1, 1937
Jonesboro, N.C.

Dear Queen Elizabeth,
    I am the eleven
year old girl with
long braids.
    You promised me
an autographed
souvenir program of
Lost Colony. But we
left soon and I did not
get to see you again.
    I want to show it
to my classmates
when school starts.
And I will always
treasure it.
    I saw the "Lost
Colony twice. I will
always remember it.
I am looking forward
to telling my school class
about it. Yours Truly
          Elaine Patton

To my baby
Florence
God bless you
always
Effie ann

Jan 29

And one that I haven't got on.

I've a lovely one made of red satin
That came from an old Dublin store.
But the point that I'm at
Is that underneath that
I haven't got on anymore.

And I had leotards on. But now when I do it, I'm in men's long red underwear.

I played the Palace and everything on the western vaudeville, and at the finish I wound up being a dramatic woman playing the part of Queen Elizabeth in *The Lost Colony* in North Carolina. I was scared to death, all those long words, you know, but I made it for two years. That was in 1937 and 1938. I rehearsed in Duke University and was in bed at 9 o'clock every night, no gallivanting around. Now I love to gallivant and play bingo or the horses. When I played Queen Elizabeth, I shook hands with our late President Roosevelt and he kissed my hand, and I presented him with a program up in the box. He also gave me a Sir Walter Raleigh coin as a present, which is worth about $40 now. There were only 350 inhabitants in that town, but when I came to the show there were 3,900 people. The president was there on August 18, 1937. Actually, my hand was kissed every night because I was the queen. I lived in the hotel and we used to play poker and my chair was Queen Elizabeth's. Nobody could take that chair. It was only penny ante, but we had a lot of fun.

Do you remember Fred Allen? He was always very good to vaudevillians or to anybody, for that matter. And he gave me a chance on his show. I was on his show three times. The first time I was in the audience and he said, can you sing, I said yes. He then asked me what I was going to sing. So I said, "I've Loved You Ever Since You Were a Baby, Laddie!" He said, Oh, I didn't know you loved me that long.

Once I hurt myself performing. I was doing my wedding act in 1943 and a young dancer came over to me before my act and said, Lillian, take care, the floor is very slippery. They had just waxed the floor. Now I had no time to do anything about it, they were already playing my introduction. So out I go to the wedding march and BOOM. I fell down right on my back. Well, the audience thought it was in the act and they're all laughing. So I twisted myself over and whispered to the orchestra, I hurt myself. But they thought it was in the act, too. Well, finally four men had to come and pick me up and take me to Bellevue.

Here's a story about the Copacabana. They were having an amateur night with Joe Lewis as master of ceremonies. I was there to perform but before, I went up to ask him for his autograph. He says, why sure, dear. Then he looked at me and says, my God, Lillian Ashton, what are you doing here? And he gave me away with that. I was supposed to be an amateur. And he hadn't seen me since 1933.

In 1949 and 1950, I traveled all over with a USO show doing a single act as a comedienne. I could really write a book on the USO shows we did. We did some shows in an insane asylum with Willie Sole, and Will Oakland, a great singer who had his own nightclub. Well, all they used to give us there in the morning was beans and I couldn't eat beans. So, one morning we decided to go out and get some eggs or something. So the three of us got together, Will Oakland with his frock coat and silk hat, little Willie with two odd shoes on, and I with a wedding dress over my arm. But when we went to leave, they stopped us at the door and said, where are you going? We told them we were with the Gay Nineties show. Get back to your cells, they yelled. They thought we were patients! We never

14

did get any breakfast that morning.

We worked a lot of wards in insane asylums and prisons and all. Another time the same thing happened to me again. After doing a show, I went up to get my feet worked on by a chiropodist in one of the asylums. I had my wedding hat and dress on, and as I sat down to get my feet done, the warden came out and said, get back to your cell. It was really funny.

I had an old withered rose that I wore in the wedding sketch, and one of the boys in the insane asylum sent me a little tobacco pouch with 85 cents in it to buy a real flower. I still have the little pouch.

I've also been on "What's My Line?" on television twice, and Arlene Francis always guessed. In 1969, I had a small part in the movie *Where's Poppa?* I made a lot of friends doing that movie.

I also make up songs. Here's my hippie song:

Look at me and you will see
An old maid hippie past 83
I'm all done and never had a beau
I'm always lonesome and forlorn
I really wish I never was born
I never look for trouble
And no trouble troubles me
But I'm a hippie old maid
Eighty-three in the shade

Never, never, never had a chance in my life
To have a nice old hippie ask to make me his wife.
Now I think that I'll stay single
For to marry I'd be afraid
I've got plenty of wealth
And I'm in good health
But I'm a hippie old maid.
But you should have seen me when I was 21,
When I was 21,
I was as fair as the rosebuds, you see.
All the boys made a fuss over me
As to who could win a smile
They'd fuss and they'd kick up a row
No one would miss me
Any chance to kiss me.
But nobody kisses me now.
I'm still a hippie, an old maid hippie,
I'm H-I-P-P-I-E.

I made up another song just recently,

Something to be thankful for
Each and everyone
Let's count our blessings
One by one
And treasure them and store
And ask God to give us
Peace, health and happiness
In our wide, wide world once more.

FLORENCE ASHTON

My life didn't start out too happily. While my mother was in London performing on the stage, my father was living with another woman and had me with them. That woman made me sell matches on the streets and I had to sleep on the floor. I can vaguely remember all that, but I do remember clearly how happy I was to be back with my mother again.

Then we sailed for America in 1911 to Newport, Rhode Island. My mother bought a home there, but my stepfather drank a lot and I remember my mother would hide me up in the bedroom when he was drunk. His people didn't like me and said because my mother was an actress, she was no good, and I shouldn't call his mother, grandma. So Mom put me in a convent. When I was baptized a Catholic in the convent, my stepfather didn't even show up, he was drunk. I remember years later, when I was playing at the Palace with my husband around 1940, my stepfather was at the stage entrance. He couldn't believe it was me all grown up.

I stayed in the convent till I was 14. I had every intention of becoming a nun. That's the way it was. But then, when I was 14, I went to visit my mother in New York, and I never went back. Mom introduced me to George White and he told me to come over to the Liberty and he would make a showgirl out of me. I hadn't had a dancing lesson in my life, but I became one of the six showgirls in the *George White Scandals*. He had trouble about my age, of course. Then when he went on the road, I went to the Follies and the stage manager picked me out. I was a gawky kid with long stringy blonde hair, and he said Mr. Ziegfeld would like to meet me. So I brought

pictures of myself from the *George White Scandals* and came in my practice clothes the next day. The stage manager said to me, I have a compliment for you, Miss Ashton. Mr. Ziegfeld says you resemble Billie Burke in profile. So I rehearsed and rehearsed and when it came time to sign contracts, they only offered $40 a week and I had been getting $75 a week from George White. But the stage manager said to me, and I'll never forget those words, "But look, if you sign with Ziegfeld, you may marry a millionaire." Those were his words, but I said, no thank you. I was a fresh kid and I walked out and went right into another show with Sam Harris in *Honey Girl*. Then from there I went back to George White, from him to Al H. Woods and *The Pink Slip* show, from there to Arthur Hammerstein and *Wildflower*. The costumes in those shows were beautiful and they cost hundreds of dollars. Broadway was beautiful then, too. No more. I was also with Peggy

Wood in a show and she took me out of the chorus and made me her maid, a little French maid at the Broadhurst Theatre in New York. I was in that show for 10 months. Peggy Wood was a wonderful woman.

I was with Willie Mae Brady in *Up She Goes*. I played the principal part in that. Then I was in a show with Heywood Broun, a lot of newspaper commentating, but it didn't last long. That was on the Century Roof called *Around the Town*. Bill Robinson taught me how to do the black-bottom dance, and I played the whole coast with him, from here to Los Angeles and back.

Then I met my husband, Harry Holmes, and fell in love. That was in 1924. He was much older than I was — 19 years older — but he was a sweetheart. A girlfriend introduced us. He had been married before and she had been in his act. After we were married, we put a big act together and played for $850 and $950 a week. We did a com-

edy act. He was a nut pianist, you know, crazy. He used to shoot me with blanks. I'd come out and sing "If I Had the Wings of an Angel," and he'd shoot me. He was a clever pianist. He could have gone to Europe and tripled his salary because he did mostly pantomime and they love that over there.

We also had a little Japanese fighting rooster in the act. His name was Joseph. We were put out of more hotels because of him. At five o'clock in the morning you can't keep a rooster from crowing. The hotel people would come up and my husband would say, oh, I'm an impersonator. In other words, he made as if he were making that crowing noise. Even on trains in a compartment, we had Joseph in a little dog box and people would say, what's going on, are we on a farm or something? They didn't know where the crowing was coming from. But you just couldn't stop him.

In the act, my husband would have Joseph on his hand and he'd say, Joseph will offer for your approval. . . . In the meantime he had this egg filled with water which he would drop and which made such a big splash that the audience would scream. Then my husband would start over, saying, Josephine will offer for your approval . . . meaning it was a female. The rooster loved my husband, he'd never let go of his fingers. We also had a skeleton in the audience lit up with radium that would scare everyone to death. We had a ball doing that act.

Then we had a black girl with us who did a reincarnation act out of a barrel. Very funny. She used to do this buck dance, no expression on her face and she'd dance her little head off. But when the Keith people bought the act, they wouldn't take her. It couldn't be black and white; it had to be one or the other. So I had to put the cork on and play the part. In Chicago I had a mask made and we broke the act in for eight or ten months before we got a break. We showed the act at the Columbia, right across from the Palace. Fred Allen was on the bill plus our act, and the audience loved it. With that we went on the road for 84 weeks straight, from here to the West Coast and back. Harry Holmes and Company.

My husband is the only man in vaudeville who would never take a bow at the end of his act. You see, once at the Palace, they laughed at the comedy, but when he sat down at the finish to play a beautiful piano solo, "The World Is Waiting for the Sunrise," no one applauded. They just didn't want anything serious from him.

From then on, he would tell the audience, my act has no finish, I'm done, good-bye, and he'd walk off the stage. He was such a good comedian, it broke my heart when he wouldn't take the All-American bill in England. He would have tripled his salary, but he didn't want to leave his folks in Atlantic City. We were once in England, we played the Palladium in London for five weeks and they loved it. I wanted to go back so bad, but he wouldn't take it. We didn't really need the money, we had our own open car, our own chauffeur, but those days are over. When he died in 1965, he didn't have a dime.

We had parted long before that, but he would never give me a divorce. I loved him but he got mixed up with another woman, in fact, the girl who introduced us. But you know how it is in show business. I could tell you a lot of stories.

When I was young I had millionaires after me and everything. In the movies, too, I had big directors after me, but I was only a kid then, and they all wanted to get fresh.

Al Smith once told me to move away from my mother and he'd put me up in a nice apartment. That's the God's truth. When I told my mother what happened, she went to him and threatened him with a gun. It wasn't a real gun, but it scared him to death. And one fellow, I'll never forget, I went up to this movie office for a part in this picture, and this guy says to me in the office, I'll give you $100 if I can kiss your breast. Well, this place had winding staircases all the way down this big movie office, and I got out of there and I never stopped running till I got home. I never got that part or anything. Three shows I was let out of because I wouldn't let the producer fool around with me.

I had a big millionaire—oh, what a big millionaire he was. All of us would go up to his apartment and he had a $50 gold piece under each plate. He wanted to put me through dancing school and make a star out of me. Nothing fresh or anything. He must have been about 70 years old and I was about 15, but of all the girls, he liked me the best. But I couldn't do it. If I had my life to live over, I'd do the same thing. Then I had a big lawyer who was in love with me and he followed me to Atlantic City and everything. He was in the cafe that night when I got engaged to Harry. He couldn't believe I was going to marry Harry. I was about 19 then. But I had to marry out of love. Unfortunately, I fell in love with the wrong man.

Let me tell you about some of the crazy times I had while I was married. One time, Vesta Wallace had had an argument with the fellow she was working with, so Leo Carrillo, the movie star, said, come on, let's go to Hollywood. So we got in a car and went up to this beautiful apartment and when we got in, there was champagne everywhere and there must have been about 15 bedrooms. And what do you know, in each of these bedrooms were big directors with Chinese girls, Japanese girls, American girls, all beautiful and all taking dope, pipes you know. One director was after me in the living room and Harry took a sock at him. I said to Vesta, let's get out of here. I saw what was going on, and we got out of there quick. That was about five in the morning and we stood waiting for one and a half hours for a cab to take us back to Los Angeles.

This story is funny. Once we were playing the Palace Theatre on Broadway and my husband always had a few drinks in him, you know, because he was funnier that way. So this one time, after the acts were finished, we saw this big police horse standing in the stage entrance all alone. So Harry says to me to get on the horse and he'll bring me into the Somerset Hotel where we were living. I said, not me, so he got another girl from the show and took the horse with Nellie on his back, up four steps into the lobby and the horse did its potatoes all over the lobby. Well, we were put out of that hotel on account of it and we had lived there for months and months. He was crazy. A lot of fun, but crazy.

I love show business. I wouldn't want to do anything else. I still do what I can. I worked as an extra in the movie, *The French Connection,* awhile back. And I take care of my mother, who is 82 years old now. I have a lot of wonderful memories.

I've been a cashier, off and on for 17 years, at different movie theaters. All they show now are sex movies, but I never watched, I just did my job as a cashier. The hours were from five to midnight. The last job was Friday and Saturday till three in the morning, very late hours. I started out as a cashier at regular movies, but everything went to sex. A cashier's job is all right, but not for sex movies. I don't like that.

SALLY DEMAY

I did an act called Demay, Moore & Martin, for many years, two gentlemen and myself. One of the gentlemen was my husband, and we did a comedy dancing act for years. We went all over the world with it. We did a command performance in England for the king and queen. We played in Germany right before World War II, around 1938 and 1939. We played in Paris, in Dover, in Monte Carlo, all the most beautiful places. We even played Rumania.

Of course, when World War II broke out, the boys had to go into the army, so I went out on my own as a single. I did a stand-up comedy act. Then I started studying acting. Later, my husband and I did a double comedy act, but in 1961 my husband decided he had had it in show business, so he went behind the scenes in show business. He heads a juvenile delinquent program with Joey Adams, and in this program they have a big show once a year in which they raise their funds. The money is used in high de-

linquent areas to teach underprivileged children the arts of show business. They hire actors to teach acting, singers to teach singing, dancers, puppeteers, everything that involves show business. I was one of his first teachers, so I did it for free and I'd go in a blizzard to teach dancing, because that was my forte at the time. Right now the program is 11 years old. Everyone is interested in it now, Rockefeller, the mayor, and my husband does a fantastic job.

When my husband left show business I went into acting, and my first starring role and first big show was *Li'l Abner.* I did Mammy Yokum in that and my write-up was — they called me a special delight veteran actress. Well, I wasn't a veteran actress, I was a dancer, but that's what they called me.

Originally, I started out as a ballerina, then I went into ballroom dancing and married my husband when I was 16. I'm still married to him, which is a long time. I met him in dancing school when I was learning ballet. He was teaching while he was going to college and I was going to high school. And we started to do an act together. I remember once, he said to me, you keep in touch with me, I might be able to use you — and he's been using me ever since. No, I'm just kidding, but that's how we met.

Now, I've gone on to do many fine things. I've done *How Now, Dow Jones,* two years ago on Broadway for David Merrick. I played a Wall Street widow with three other ladies and when the show was over, those ladies and I formed an act called the Wall Street Widows. We played all the top TV shows, Merv Griffin, Mike Douglas, David Frost, the Sullivan Show, we even got to do the Tony Awards. They picked the number we did in the show on the Tony Awards. My big money-maker now is commercials. I had a Doan's Pill commercial on the air and it ran for three years. Right now, I have one on the air called Tootsie Pop Drops. It's on only in the morning for children.

So I've had quite a career, when you see that I went from a trio, to a single, to a double, to a single, into the legitimate field, because I think I saw the trend of vaudeville coming. I think I kind of used my head when I went to study acting. A lot of vaudevillians didn't make the transition, I guess, because they couldn't see ahead and maybe they didn't realize that there were other ends of the business they could take a step forward in. You see, when I was a youngster and I heard the word modeling, I thought you had to be beautiful to do modeling. Now, I'm a tiny person and I'm not beautiful. However, I'm now doing modeling and I get the same money as the highest-priced models. I model for automobiles, for tires, I model for pharmaceutical people, pills, etc. As a matter of fact, I just modeled a new thing that's coming out, a new rocking chair made out of chrome and I play Whistler's Mother. I'm dressed in a dark brown wig and, by golly, I look just like Whistler's Mother. It's very funny.

I've been in show business since 1929, since I was a little girl. So I got into the vaudeville end of it. I did the two-a-day. I played the Palace, all the Loew's theaters, the RKO theaters, I played what they called the Interstate time, like through Texas and Oklahoma, everywhere.

I don't live in my memories, though, and I won't. I'll tell you why. I don't waste my time on yesterday. My philosophy of life is, live for today. Now, what tomorrow brings is another story. Today is the day I got to be doing things. I don't know if I felt like that when I was 16, but that's the way I've felt in recent years. Some people get depressed about things, and I say, don't. One door will close, but there's always another door that'll open if you let it. I, more or less, try to see the bright side of things. There

30

are times when you get a little discouraged, of course, but you have to try and look at the bright side.

We live in Manhattan, but we used to live in Forest Hills in our house till the war broke out. I'll tell you, for our business, it's good to live in the Times Square area to get where you're going in 15 or 20 minutes. Living in Forest Hills was beautiful for a home life. We had a garden, we had a home if you know what I mean, but I think for show people, and as the years pass and there's just the two of you, and if you're still going strong, I think it's good to live in Manhattan.

I never had children, I was in vaudeville all my life and never had time for children, but I did raise my two brothers. My mother died when I was just 15, so I more or less raised my two younger brothers. Now they're married and have children of their own. One has four boys, and the other has two boys. So I sort of help them go through college. So God's been good to me. I wrote a record ten years ago called "Smokum Yokum" while I was doing Mammy Yokum. It's all about Mammy coming to the big city and I tell how she gets on a plane for the first time and how she was frightened and so on. I just got the idea and I did it with a hillbilly dialect.

I've worked with Milton Berle, I've worked on bills with Donald O'Connor, who to this very day is our dearest friend. I used to make coffee for him in his dressing room. We worked with a lot of beautiful people. Last season, I understudied six roles in *70 Girls 70*. They said I was too young, so they let me understudy six roles. It was fantastic, but I'll never do it again. It was too much work. Last year, I did an off-Broadway show called *Cold Feet*, but the critics didn't like the show. But they liked me. They said, I provoked genuine laughter. Anyway, we're trying.

I can say I'm not sorry for a minute of it. I've had disappointments, of course. It took me seven years to get my first commercial, but when I did, I really went strong. I've done 34 so far. I had 6 Scope commercials, 6 for Macy's, and I've done all kinds of characters.

I'd advise kids to study all facets of show business, all the facets, and I recommend it highly.

FRED ESTELLE

My career started in 1906 at Dreamland, Coney Island, as a magician. Dreamland at that time was one of the star places to play. I can remember Bustock, the famous animal trainer having his arm torn off by a lion. My first week's pay there was $75. My stepfather, who worked as head chef in Riggs Restaurant on 34th Street and Sixth Avenue got $18 a week. So the first week I came home and gave my mother $50 and kept $25 for myself. My stepfather, who was a strict German, says, okay, where did you steal it. I said, I beg your pardon, Pop, I didn't steal it, I earned it. He wanted to know who would be paying me that kind of money, so I told him to come out to Coney Island on his day off. Well, he did, and saw me up on the platform escaping out of a straitjacket. I was his pet son. I had a brother and sister, but after that, I was his favorite. I'd come home every week with $50 and I'd say, here Mom, spend it. Money don't mean a damn thing in life, unless you don't have it. And when you do have it, it don't mean anything either because they take it away one way or another. . .

Oh, I could tell you lots of stories. Once I was playing in St. Louis and we were on a program with an elephant. The elephant's name was Baby Helen and all the music publishers in New York used to send her copies of their music for her to sing. One Sunday afternoon, I'm standing at the entrance to the stage and the elephant is parked outside in the alleyway with a chain, of course, waving her trunk. I thought, uh oh, that elephant is mad. And sure enough, the manager came up after having his dinner and he wanted to pass the elephant. She grabbed him around the neck and drove a tusk into his neck. She didn't kill him, but she was impounded by the police and the trainer was arrested. The elephant was used to free lunch during the week and the saloons were closed on Sundays, and she was spoiled during the week. . .

I'm not performing now because I'm 80 years old. My wife passed away at 75. We were married 54 years. I was born and raised in New York.

I went from coast to coast numerous times playing the same act for 25 years, without a change. In the beginning, I usually had a male partner, but later on my wife became my partner in the act which we called The Estelles.

Harry Blackstone and I were supposed to go and work double for a while, but it didn't pan out. Then Houdini featured me a few times. They were preparing to put on a big show on the road and I was supposed to be the star of that, but Houdini died before it was finished. That was in 1926.

When Sir Arthur Conan Doyle came from London, Harry Houdini said he wanted me to appear for Sir Arthur. He was a great believer in spiritualism, you see. So they engaged the Sullivan Theater, which is now a pony house on 42nd Street, for a Sunday night. Sir Arthur was coming here to lecture on spiritualism, on some of the real phenomena he believed in, and I was used as a foil to prove that all of these things were not genuine. I know they're not genuine. After all, I've been a faker all my life. . .

In my act, we also reproduced what apparently were spirit flowers which we'd throw into the audience. Once when I played in Boston, Mrs. Mary Baker Eddy came backstage to discuss these flowers and I said, no, Mrs. Eddy, I wouldn't fool you. I told her those flowers were bought on the market. She actually thought they were really spirit flowers. We have been approached by so many people wanting to know about the flowers. Of course, I won't tell you how we produced them. I'm a professional magician. Our code of ethics in the Magical Society is never to expose what we do. No magician will ask another how he does his particular tricks. Of course, everyone knows there's no such thing as the supernatural. Well, then again, there must be *something* to it since Duke University is doing so much investigating. They put up a special building there just for the purpose of reproducing these effects and analyzing various supernatural feats. But I haven't been following it too much anymore. I've lost the use of one eye and the other is going, so I can't read much now.

How did I become a magician? Well, I did all my studying at home. I saw a magician when I was ten. My father was in the German hotel business for German theatrical people who came to New York. They stopped at my father's place at 211 Chrystie Street. We had a magician there. He did a couple of tricks and I liked it so much, I

followed it up. Gradually, piece by piece, I got my skills together. My favorite trick was the spirit flower trick. That was my meal ticket and I put my daughter through college with it. She ended up with five degrees with math as her major. She was studying to be a math teacher, but O'Brien, the mayor of New York, reduced the staff of teachers in the city, so she worked for the Social Security Administration for 32 years and now she's retired. But that flower reproduction made her education possible. I used between 150 and 200 fresh flowers every day, all kinds of flowers which I bought at a wholesaler. . .

Times Square now is terrible. You used to be able to walk anywhere, any time. I can even remember when the Bowery was the theatrical center of the city.

Looking back, I made a lot of good friends. I've had a lot of wonderful experiences. You must be able to take the good with the bad. To me, they were all good times because the bad ones never bothered me a bit. I have a very busy time now doing nothing. By the time I get to bed, I'm tired. I shop, I eat breakfast at home in my little apartment. During the day I stop out and eat my supper. Once in a while, I take my daughter out to dinner or one of my friends. So I'm at liberty all the time. I even refuse engagements. This year they wanted me on a Christmas show for a children's party which I used to do, but I turn them all down. I don't want to make a circus of myself, because if you can't see, you can't do that sort of thing anymore. Moving around the way we did, there wasn't much security, but I feel as though it has given me an education which I couldn't have gotten from any college. I saw things around the country, I listened, and I learned. I never learned anything out of a book, because you couldn't have much of an education if you started to work at 13 years of age.

NONA OTERO
KATHERINE MURRAY
HARRIET WALDRON

Muriel Finley

ZIEGFELD
GIRLS

Nona Otero

HARRIET: I am very happy to tell my age. I am a senior citizen and I never did think that I would live this long to be this happy to become a senior citizen. I have had a lot of fun and my husband was a real wonderful man. He was a Shepherd of the Lambs Club and he passed away in 1969 and I miss him greatly. He was very annoyed that I was doing so much work for the Ziegfeld Club because I didn't get home until very late and he said, Ziegfeld Girls? —I don't know why you call yourselves Ziegfeld Girls; all I can say you were girls when Chinatown only had one chink. The first Ziegfeld Follies was in 1906. Of course, we are of a much later vintage quite obviously.

I did all sorts of good work on the stage. I was an ingenue, I followed Ina Claire in *Paper Girl* and then Julie Sanderson in *The Girl from Utah* and then I had a contract with Ziegfeld in 1926 and then I went to the Palladium in London. I did vaudeville for quite a long time. I did the Keith Orpheum circuits. I sang and I danced— you'd never know it now.

HARRIET: My stage name was Miss Harriet. Well, I worked not only for Ziegfeld but I worked for Shubert for many years. I worked in *Rain or Shine* with Joe Cook and then I went to Europe, worked at the Moulin Rouge, the Casta Mio. Then I took a troupe of girls called the Harriet Girls and I took them to South America. Some of the girls that I had were much older. I was a little young to have authority and to handle girls. However, I managed and I made a lot of money and I figured that money was very important. I was never a person who thought it was all glamour. Because I was brought up in Philadelphia where they had building and loan and insurance, I figured I had to make money. I wasn't in show business for glamour. I was in it strictly to make money. . .

NONA: I couldn't agree less. I don't agree with that at all. I think it's an education in itself. The contacts you make, the travel you do. First of all we are trained how to talk, how to sing and how to conduct yourself. No, I think it is like going to college twice over.

HARRIET: Well, if you had a daughter, would you want her in show business?

NONA: Well, I don't know about show business, how it is today. First of all I don't go along with this nudity business. It's not because I'm a prude but I do say this: where do you go from there? I mean, you still have to know something about your craft. I think you have to know something about the theater and not just stand there and take your clothes off and say—here I am. That's the whole thing. . .

38

I think it was much more colorful in my day with the big raccoon coats, the stage johnnies, the flowers. You don't have stage johnnies anymore. The young boys today if they want to take a girl out, they can't afford to put aside $50 because before an evening is over for dinner and show, it runs $50. In the old days you used to go out for $15 and have a real ball and when they would take you to the door and say, may I kiss you good night, and oh, that was a real vice — and you say, well, should I or shouldn't I? . . .

KATHERINE: I'm glad we lived when we did and not now. It was a much more charming life than it is now. People had money then, they wore evening clothes and high hats and went to theaters and it was glamorous. Today they wear turtle-neck sweaters. . .

NONA: I was so shocked when Dennis King died the other day. You know, I was in *The Three Musketeers* with him. At the time I used to stand in the wings every night and watch him. I had such a crush on that man, unbelievable. Don't tell my husband. I was a youngster — that was a long, long time ago. But I watched him during every single show. I used to stand in the wings with my mouth open. I don't know what he thought of the whole thing. I never really approached him, you know, just watched from a distance. He was the king, he was a very handsome man. He died last year.

HARRIET: We had a different sort of life. I would many times get up at 6 a.m. in the morning and go horseback riding in Central Park. We were all very young and we had a lot of fun. Everything was a highlight. We had to go to the beauty parlor and all these things. I never seemed to have time to sleep. I used to get very tired and many times no one could find me. I

used to be up in the balcony at the Amsterdam or the Shubert Theatre. People would say, I wonder where Harriet is? Oh, she is up sleeping. I would just fall asleep. I would sleep on a makeup shelf or anyplace because I was really tired. I did acrobatic work. I did fencing, climbed ropes, all kinds of things. The work was not easy, and we never had any social life.

NONA: I don't think most people realize how little social life theater girls have — dancers or performers in the theater — because we put all our energies and all our time in either performing or studying. We studied for hours and hours from daybreak. We went from one lesson to another. We were all essentially dancers. Dancing we all loved. . . .

KATHERINE: The most wonderful thing I had was vaudeville. When I was in the

Keith Orpheum circuit, I played under Sarah Bernhardt. It was her last visit and she did the dying scene in *Camille*. I used to stand in the wings and watch her every performance and she used to say to me — You come right out, dear, and stand any-place you want and watch me. I started when I was 17. I met my husband when I was playing at the Palladium in London and they held me over for four weeks. I had a week off and I decided to go to Paris. I went to Chateau Madrid which is a great place for Grand Prix tea in the afternoon and I had a letter of introduction to a man and a woman over there and my husband was their nephew, and so I met him at the Chateau Madrid and he asked me to marry him that night.

NONA: Isn't that interesting? It took my husband a whole week to propose to me and your husband proposed the first night. . . . I think one of the bonds we have, Kay, is that your husband always treated you like my husband treats me — like a little girl.

HARRIET: Jack never treated me like a lit-tle girl. I used to take care of him like he was a little boy. Now I'm looking for some-one the other way. I don't want anyone to take care of. I am not like these other widows saying I'll never get married again. If I find the right person, believe me, I'll get married again. I'm very lonesome. My husband was 14 years older. He would be close to 80 now. He didn't have a day of sickness. . . . We had evening clothes hang-ing on the door right before he died. He had two tuxedos and I had a change of evening clothes and we were out every night and his death came as such a shock. I am very lonesome.

KATHERINE: Put an ad in the paper.

NONA: Well, with all your pep and energy, Harriet, it won't be long.

HARRIET: I don't know whether I could find anyone like Jack.

NONA: You won't find anyone like Jack, dear, but you'll find a nice companion if you are really serious.

KATHERINE: Oh no, I don't want to ever remarry. I had too happy a life.

HARRIET: But you have Anna. She brought her maid back from Switzerland 17 years ago. She has Anna to take care of her and then she has her chauffeur downstairs. She has all these things going for her. I don't. She has her bed turned down for her. I stayed there and my bed was turned down. It's a pleasure. I am tired of doing things for myself.

KATHERINE: Well, I have an old-fashioned kind of maid. They don't do those things anymore. She undresses me every night and hangs my clothes up, puts my clothes out in the morning and turns my bath on.

HARRIET: See, I don't have any of this.

KATHERINE: One of my main interests is the Ziegfeld Club and we are trying to make it larger so we can make more money for the poor and unfortunate people whom we help.

HARRIET: We have so many cases and we do it all anonymously. For example, we have the Ziegfeld secretary, her name is Katherine Dicks Wildey. She is in the Jew-ish Memorial Hospital. We are all writing to her and visiting her. We just had to put away six of her cats and a dog. She had twelve cats, she was ashamed of having so many. She couldn't breathe, the cats were taking all the oxygen. But the funny thing is, to have the dog put away costs $15 be-cause the dog is fat. So I'm going to watch my weight. And then the girl who was taking care of the cats had an infection, the cat scratched her. These are the little things we do. These things you can't mention ac-tually if someone asks what do you do and we say, well we put cats away. But these

are the things that come up that we have to do. There are so many of our ladies that need help. . .

(Phone rings)

HARRIET: Oh, my God, isn't that terrible. John Steel, the most famous Ziegfeld tenor. John Steel passed away today. He was one of the greatest stars the Follies ever had. He made famous "A Pretty Girl Is Like a Melody." It's a great loss to show business because he was one of the greatest stars Ziegfeld ever had. I'm silly crying, but you see I'm Irish, and I'm very emotional.

ELEANOR CODY HARRIET WALDRON

HARRIET: It seems I was always with the showgirls. Every time they went out I was trying to figure out where I could go 'cause they seemed to be having more fun. And I was always interested in having fun so I went out as 23 when I was 15. I went out on parties and would come home a little late and my grandma would say — what happened, and I would say — Nanny, I was rehearsing, tsk, tsk, tsk. It was real pleasurable and I think there were very many other girls doing the same thing because we were so strictly prohibited against hav-

ing to do with these things and I think we all decided we were going to do it—it was just like being told you shouldn't smoke in those days. . . .

ELEANOR: I went back to acting full time about three or four years ago, gave up everything, gave up directing, gave up teaching and producing, and I have had more fun, I wish I had done it years ago—you know.

HARRIET: Well, you have—you retired to have your family—

ELEANOR: Yes, exactly, then I went back in. And I have two films running now I want you to know. Well, I have a singing part in *Husbands* with John Cassavetes and then I played a very aristocratic mother of a girl who's in love with Lenny Bruce, in the film *Dirty Mouth*. And the daughter takes her to a cabaret to catch his act, and of course, she was just horrified and tells him so when she meets him and walks out on him. And then she is the one who is responsible for starting the obscenity cases against him—you see, to save her daughter she attacks this guy—gets him jailed, and I don't blame her!

HARRIET: The last *Sunday News* went into great details about the whole life story about Leonard Bruce and how far advanced he was compared to today and everything that he said like ten years ago, they're saying it today, but they're saying it doubly strong. Four-letter words now are not rejected and I don't think he did this to be an exhibitionist. This is the way he felt it. . . I thought he had talent. When he took his case to court he said all he wanted to do—I mean, last words he said before dying—let me do my act. . .

I began my career when I first met a woman named Gertrude Hoffman, a very famous dancer. I joined her dance company in Philadelphia and we came to New York, and first we worked for the Shu-

berts. That was in 1921 and then in 1922 we worked for the Keith circuit and in 1923 we went in the Follies for Mr. Ziegfeld and in 1924, Miss Hoffman took us to Europe, London first. In Paris we worked at the Moulin Rouge for one year and that year I saw a boy standing in the hallway who was very handsome and beautiful. And I was very young and I said—I don't know who he is but I'm going to marry him.

46

That's the truth, and I did. . .

Let me tell you something interesting about my grandmother. We were making a very good salary, you know, with Hoffman, and I remember my grandmother loved it very much — we used to have these big nights, she used to buy champagne for all the mothers, big dolls, but she was really kicking up her heels, high on champagne and all these dolls for all the mothers, she

was really a delightful lady.

Now her main reason for coming with me to London was that she had told my grandfather that she must definitely go because she was going to look up her family and not a word was said. She was leaving London to go to Paris with me, so she said, Pet, would you do me a favor, and I said, what, Nanny. We never had told a lie to each other in our lives. She said, if you don't mind let's not tell Grandpa that I didn't go to look up my brothers and sisters because, she said, you know they wouldn't be there, would they, dear. And I said, no, Nanny, no, they wouldn't have been. And she never did look up her family. Her main reason to get out of Philadelphia was to travel and to be with me and we had a dancer, Leon Barte and he used to take her to all the antique shops and she was a very old woman.

HARRIET: Oh, I came back and I was in a show called *Rain or Shine* and then I started to do a little vaudeville with a dancer named William Seebury and his act had broken up and there was a very clever agent then named Tony Shane. He says Harriet, I want you to meet Jack Waldron, I want you to work with him, so I went into the rehearsal hall and I saw Jack Waldron and he kept his hat on, so I thought, he must be baldheaded or something and he wasn't at all. In the rehearsal halls in those days the men used to keep their hats on — you know. So then I started to work with Jack and did all of that — comedy together and I did the dancing and the singing and everything — and my grandmother liked him. She liked him most of all because he stayed in this country, and he was very much older and when I married Jack he was 40. He had never been married before. So I went to Chicago, I married him and we had a very happy life, and a very wonderful man.

The songs of the days that I was with Jack? Well the song that I had with Henri was "Lovers" by Berlin which was my theme song and with Jack we had some crazy songs like — he used to play the piano a little bit on the black keys — we used to do a thing, "Last Time I'll Shake It under the Sheets with You."

Real crazy vaudeville songs. You see, we were not what you'd call artistic people. We made a lot of money in vaudeville and we had a lot of fun. Eleanor met Jack but she didn't get to know him too well, because he passed on shortly after. Jack had the most brilliant mind of any man that I've ever met. He was great in the PR business. Well, every other day he was in Wilson's column and he knew all of the newspapermen. He knew all of the detectives and he knew all of the gangsters so I used to say — what are you playing — cops or robbers? And he knew everyone in Chicago. That's the reason I have all those files there and there are a few that would like to write his life story, which would be a very interesting life story.

ELEANOR: I had a life with a very fascinating man, too. Well, again this sounds absolutely crazy. I met him at a party in Carnegie Hall and he did the same thing. He told the man he was with that I was the girl he was going to marry and the very first date we had, he proposed to me and I accepted. And I was engaged to two other men at the time.

HARRIET: You were a little fickle, weren't you.

ELEANOR: I was a terrible flirt. But I was just in love with everybody. But he was the one that was the most persistent. Six months later we got married. He was a very fine artist. . . .

And Famous Players — I could just go across the street and work in the studio. I worked for Metro, I worked for Universal — all in New York. I have almost no stills — I would give anything if I had, but I just didn't bother to get them. You know, I worked with Gloria Swanson, I worked with Mae Clarke, I worked with Alice Brady and Marion Davies and all the great stars, and I don't have any pictures.

HARRIET: Oh, you have very wonderful memories.

ELEANOR: Yes, I have wonderful memories but it would be fun to have the stills so that I could have a record of it. As I told you though, my memories are so hazy of my whole past life. . . .

One thing I remember about the Twenties — I mean the early Twenties was how much we danced. You'd go someplace for lunch and you danced and then you'd go to a tea dance. "Tea Dansant" as they called them. I remember Mac Murray's restaurant had a circular floor with mirrors all around and the floor kept circling as you danced. You would go for lunch and you would dance all the time you were eating.

HARRIET: It only cost around $3 or $4.

ELEANOR: I don't even know what it cost. In those days I always had an escort. And there was a place called the Club Devrne, remember? and we'd all go there every afternoon and then we'd go out to dinner and we'd dance. Wherever you went, you danced. It doesn't seem to me that they have the fun we used to have. We spent our lives dancing. If we weren't dancing in a show, we were dancing in a cabaret someplace, having fun. All day long. All night long!

HARRIET: Now I've tried recently to go places — but I'm thinking about the time to get home. I don't want to get home too late. I have to get my keys out and you know — you have to worry about getting into your building because now I'm really slightly frightened and I haven't really any fear but, people do put fear into you.

48

ELEANOR: They certainly do. I remember when I had the theater and I'd come home at two every night, I didn't have time to think — I had a job to do and I did it. But I haven't had the gaiety in my life that Harriet had because I had to work so darn hard —

HARRIET: Well, honey, I worked hard too —

ELEANOR: But I mean lately, you see — lately. Teaching at the Academy and with my theater and directing plays I haven't really had time —

HARRIET: . . . To me show business was only a means to an end — I thought that you had to make money.

ELEANOR: No, I was married to an artist and art came first. Art for art's sake.

HARRIET: Well, that's a nice way to be, but I always figured in dollars and cents and when I quit — actually when I quit show business — I think it was about 1936 — about four years after I married my husband Jack, I decided I wasn't getting anyplace. It would be easier for me to sit home and let him earn the money. And that's exactly what I did. Of course, then I didn't have any money to put in the bank, but that didn't bother me because I wasn't doing anything. I still don't believe in giving your services free. . . .

ELEANOR: I love to do parts you know, completely opposite to myself because then if you're playing someone so completely opposite to yourself, you're much less self-conscious. The closer you are to your own character in a part, the more difficult it is to do. But when you get completely away and play a part that's completely different from you, it's much easier. I like to do funny old ladies — peasant women. I did the mother in *Tobacco Road* and had a perfectly lovely time doing it. I would die onstage every night, you know, it's the dream of an actor to die onstage —

HARRIET: Which act, the first act?

ELEANOR: The last act, oh no, I'm on all through the play —

HARRIET: Oh, I always wanted to die in the first act so I could get home early.

ELEANOR: Listen to her.

HARRIET: I wanted that because I would get paid for doing just one act and I could go home and that would be it. Then I could double in something else.

ELEANOR: Isn't she wonderful. I also did Marty in *Anna Christie,* the old Tugboat Annie part that Marie Dressler played. And those parts I just adored to do, you know, these tough old broads. Something interesting happened to me in *Tobacco Road.* I grew up in West Virginia and when we were kids we learned the mountain dialect, we would do it as a stunt — well, I thought I'd forgotten it but it was all in my subconscious and when I did *Tobacco Road* every bit of that dialect came back to me. It was very interesting. I didn't know it was all stored up there in my subconscious mind. That's one of the fascinating things about acting and directing. Everything you've ever experienced in your whole life you can use at one time or another in a character you're creating. Nothing's lost, it's always there waiting for you to use it. . . .

HARRIET: The most interesting showgirl I ever met was Hilda Ferguson. She died — she had a very unhappy finish — she was an extremely generous girl. She has a daughter who married very well — trying to think of the name of the man she married — very wealthy man — I call her young Hilda. She doesn't really look anything like her mother, she isn't half as beautiful as Hilda — she did a number in the Follies called "Whoops, I'm an Indian" and any of the girls that cared to go out at that time, if they wanted to borrow her mink wrap, whatever she had, she would lend them very gladly. She was one of the nicest girls I've ever met, but some of the showgirls

were very interesting in the Follies.

Ziegfeld, of course, was very strict. He did not want his — he called them his women or his gals — he didn't want them out. But that would be just like calling a revolution because, I mean, in those days we didn't have women's lib but the girls would still do as they wanted, and they still did go out even against his wishes and some of the girls were very beautiful, some of them were, I would say, a little — like we had one girl, Holly Lee Worthing, he used to dress her, he would keep her legs covered, she was — I don't mind this at all — she was knock-kneed and she had very, very skinny legs and he always dressed her as a Dresden Doll with the big Dresden skirt — from here up she was beautiful but from there down she was not so beautiful and some of the girls were really very beautiful but most of them, I would say, he created and they weren't half as beautiful as he made them because he knew all their shortcomings and he knew how to cover them or to build them up or to do something with them — and he knew nothing about comedy.

Ziegfeld never knew what to do with a comic — he didn't know whether a man was funny or not and he had some of the greatest comics, like W. C. Fields, he had Ed Wynn, he had Walter Catlett. Of course, he had Eddie Cantor and he had so many clever men, but he did not know what to do with them. He knew what to do with women. And once he had a cowboy thing in which the girls would be partially draped, he never had any nudes, they would have a little thing over here, from their left breast to their right breast, and a little thing, a circular thing on their skirts, but he made this so impressive that not even the stagehands saw these girls because they were mounted on these great big statue effects, and they were mostly always white, he had them mostly white and pink, never

had an Indian or like an outdoor type of girl, they were always pink and white, very feminine. . . .

We had very prominent men who used to sit in the wings. And Paul Block — these men were the backbone of the Ziegfeld Follies, they gave all the money. Ziegfeld, he donated nothing and he was a great deal like John Murray Anderson — you've heard of him, I'm sure. He was as close to Ziegfeld as anyone I know. He was fabulous. He put on fabulous productions. He'd say I can put that one on for $50,000. When John Murray Anderson said he could put it on for $50,000, that meant it would be $250,000 like Ziegfeld because there was never any end to the cost.

We had operalane stockings, every night they were changed. If you got a slight runner, you had a new pair of tights. The tights I think were furnished by Miller, the shoes were by Miller, the gloves were imported from France. Now after I left Ziegfeld and I worked for the Shuberts — forget it, because at the Shuberts you could wear the same pair of tights with 29 runners for a week and they couldn't have cared less and yet Shubert made money.

And actually, it was — it was a much happier family working for the Shuberts because everybody knew everybody. In the Follies you never got acquainted, you were on one floor, you never knew the people on the other floor. We had Lena Baskett and she came from a very fine family and this was her first experience as a ballerina. Fanny Brice was just divine. You could walk up to her and say — Hello, Fanny, and she would say hello and know you by name. She was the most remarkable woman in the world. Some of the women were just lovely. . . .

ELEANOR: I'm auditioning Friday morning for a faded movie star in — oh, dear, I've got it written down and I can't remember the

name of the play I'm auditioning for. It's the part of Iris. *Peninsula* is the name of it and Tammy Grimes is playing the lead in it. It's going out on the road the end of August, I think, and they're auditioning for it now. And, of course, I would love to play the part of a faded, glamorous star named Iris. But I've never seen the play so I've got to get the script and do my homework before I audition.

Oh, yes, as I told you, I'm auditioning all the time and doing films and commercials. But it's all fun and I enjoy it and the most exciting part about it, you never know what's going to happen tomorrow. That's what's such fun. Maybe tomorrow I'll be exactly the right type for the right part, be the right age and the right height and the right color. Oh, I remember one of the famous stars saying that she was out in Hollywood and had a run of bad luck and she said she was too tall or too short or too fat or too thin or too dark or too light for every part that she auditioned for. Finally there was a part that she was going to audition for that was exactly right for her and she was so excited, so she went to audition and the producer said—the only trouble is, you're just too right for this part. She didn't get it. So this is what you go through when you audition. You never know what the producer has in his mind. You know, he has a mental picture and you might be that picture and you might not be the picture. . . .

PHIL FOOTE

In November of 1971 I was living in Mansfield Hall which is at 226 West 50 Street, and on November 21, I was down on 50th and Eighth Avenue and I crossed and a car hit me on the left hip. I went to Polyclinic Hospital. They didn't know whether I was going to pull through or not but God was with me and so I did. So I stayed down there for a long time. I don't remember anything until about four days before Christmas. So then after that I was in a wheelchair for most of the time until I finally got better. I worked with my Christian Science practitioner because as it happens, I go to the Christian Science Church.

Along by the fourth of April, 1972, I had a chance to go to the DeWitt Nursing Home. I wanted to go to Florence Nightingale where I had played many times, but they said that the DeWitt was better and I think that the choice was good, because over there they had physical therapy, I took a little of that. But then they had a nice big place on the top where we gave concerts so it got me back playing piano again. And on January 31, 1973, I had just finished reading the newspaper after breakfast and they told me I was too healthy, that I had to leave and go home right away. Well, I says, my God, I can't do that by this time. So I happened to think of Stanley at the Park Plaza Hotel where I had stayed in 1968 and I called Stanley, he's a hell of a nice guy and a good manager, and he says, yes,

I remember you and you were a good tenant. Come on over, I've got a single for you. So at five o'clock I packed and I left the nursing home. And I did much better since that time.

Now in order to get back to work again, of course—I'm 75 years old now and when I was five years old I went on the stage, so I've actually been in the entertainment business for 70 years. I've probably written a thousand songs. I've written two musicals. I wrote a symphony. But I decided that what I wanted to do was get back to work again. So I thought that the best way to do that would be to organize Piano Phil's Ramblers and give old-fashioned, old-time jazz. I knew W. C. Handy and I'm strictly of the New Orleans school. Of course, I play classical stuff but I think what they need is that.

So about October, Stud Forster called me and says, well, what about the New York Jazz Museum; let's go down some Sunday. I says, okay, let's go and see what happens. We went down there, there were four of us. There was Stud, a fellow by the name of Stan Parker, and a fellow by the name of Big Andy who played a guitar. There weren't over 30 people there but we built that up till the crowd was about 225 and I now have about nine pieces down there. So what I'm trying to do at the present time is to give concerts at Town Hall, or whatever the case may be, and to organize my own club, which will be known as Piano Phil's. It's my idea that this must be on Broadway. There are several places that I'm going to talk to real estate people about, but I've always wanted to see my name up in lights and I think I can do a good job. Now what we will do, we can have the Piano Phil's Ramblers, and for interludes, we can have the old vaudeville dancers, or we can have some vaudevillians do their acts.

In 1924, I had a big hit in London. Before that I was out in India and we had our own theater out there. And when I came back to London, I managed to have a hit in London in 1924 called *Get Your Dancing Shoes.* And at that time I sold four out of seven songs that I had written on a weekend. So I came back to the United States and I ran into two fellows by the names of Jack Mills and Al Dubin when they were way down on 23rd Street, and I said, Al, I'd like to have you show some of my songs to Jack, maybe he'll publish them. And he says, listen, if an act isn't working it, you might as well give up. He says, a kid can come in here with a tune written on a paper bag and if vaudeville is using it, he'll take it without any further question. He says, my advice to you is to ghostwrite. I says, all right, Al, I'll take your advice.

Now Al Dubin and Harry Warner were two of the best writers for MGM for 25 years. *Golddiggers* and God knows what other musicals. So I took his advice. So what I had to do, I had to ghostwrite for people. If they wanted my name on the thing, all right, I didn't mind. But in doing that, I made $250 to $300 every time that I'd ghostwrite, which was much better than getting down on your hands and knees and being refused by publishers. So I was out in San Francisco during the hard days in 1933 when show business was—there wasn't any to be perfectly candid. And I was ghostwriting out there for anybody who'd want to pay me $10 or $15.

Well, there was an Irish woman that came in, she had a simple little Irish lyric. She wanted to know if I'd write the music, and I says, I'll take $15, because times were hard and I wanted to eat over the weekend. So I wrote a little simple ditty and she took it down to MGM in Hollywood and she ran into a fellow by the name of Victor who was one of the foremost music writers of Hollywood. He liked the little song and he said to her, we'd like to put you on the music staff because you've written good music. She confessed that she didn't write it.

Now what she should have done was to get on the phone and call me in San Francisco and I could have gone down there and been on the staff. But instead she didn't do it. When she came back, she showed me a photostat of a certified check for $1,500 that she'd gotten for the song. And if my memory serves me right, she did give me another $10. So I got $25 and she got $1,500. But all she had to do was tell them she didn't write it and I would have been on the staff in Hollywood. She disappeared completely after that. I don't know where she went and I don't care.

I was married three times. The first girl was a girl by the name of Julia, in 1920. I went to India for Standard Oil Company and I was in the foreign marketing department out there. I turned out to be an executive with a very good salary. I met Julia at 72nd Street and Riverside Drive. It was a blind date and being the polite little gentleman that I was — she was affectionate, yes, but we were married in 1926 when I came home from India. Then she turned out to be a Frigidaire. And I had a hard problem for eight years, you can bet me, at least trying to stay moral. So I had to get a divorce when I came back in 1933.

So then my second wife was one that I met in San Francisco. She was wonderful. Her name was Elizabeth Matthews. She was Elizabeth Putnam Matthews and as a matter of fact, she was one of the proud blue-bloods from up around — she was Elizabeth Putnam Putnam Matthews, if you know what I mean. But she was a published poetess. She could send stuff to the *Ladies' Home Journal* and in a week a check would come back for her. No kidding about it.

Everything went along fine as far as she was concerned, but then she passed away about two years later. And we wrote one beautiful song, it was based on Debussy's "Clair de Lune," and it was a thing called "You Are My Music." So that was a very happy thing. We were in Berkeley at the time and that was the year that I finished my Leafshower Symphony in 1937.

She was a most encouraging person because being creative herself, she didn't mind how long I stayed up at night. Any other wife would say, get the hell in bed, you know. But what she would do, she would get me milk and cookies. And I wrote the Leafshower Symphony which was a thing in four movements and it was written after a poem by Wordsworth. It was a standard symphony in four movements and in the last movement which was, of course, an allegro, I didn't like it because it didn't spark for some reason or another. Later I conducted it in the presence of Pierre Monteux with a 110-piece orchestra in San Francisco and he liked it, so much so, he wanted to repeat it with the Standard Symphony Hour, but I didn't like the thing because for some reason the last movement didn't jell. No action in it.

So we went down to Betty's mother's house in San Mateo, and I will say they were considerate people because, as I say, they were creative. So one night after dinner, for some reason I was tired, and went in and dropped off to sleep, and I had a most wonderful dream. I could see leaves coming down all over the place and when they'd come they were dipping with the wind that blew them down and that gave me the answer. So I sat up that night, she brought in cookies and everything that I needed and she and her mother went to bed, and by the next morning I had written 104 measures in the middle. It sparked the whole fourth movement. Unfortunately, the

manuscript has been lost. I think I can re-create it though.

When I was out in Oakland, a fellow ran a piano store right under the place where I had my music publishing and recording business. So Loretta, who was night-club trained, she was born in Berkeley but her mother lived up here in the northern part of New York State, she'd been in night-clubs since about 1918. Well, she needed a job and I needed some help, so she came up to me. This is before we were married. I was the first one ever to put sheet music out in the bookstores and drugstores in racks. But that business gave me a head-ache so we got out of that. Of course I had to have a truck and I had difficulties there because during the war I couldn't get gasoline.

But Loretta and I were finally married and she was a wonderful musician. She was one of the best sight readers I've ever known. She couldn't remember do-re-mi as far as memory was concerned—she played for music and she couldn't transpose. But we got along fine. The result of it was, we were on KFRC out in San Francisco with a show called "Can You Write A Song." And a fellow by the name of Sanford Dick-erson was our manager and he was the hus-band of Faith Bacon, the famous striptease dancer who invented the fan dance.

I did several good arrangements for her. In fact, when her act opened up in Seattle, I couldn't go up there with her, but the old pianist up there said, give my congratula-tions to Phil; I think that that's one of the best arrangements I've ever heard. Course, she was always fighting with Sally Rand. I played with Sally, she's tough as hell. But they were arguing as to who invented the fan dance. I'm not gonna pay any attention to it, but I think that Faith was one of the best ones.

Later I tried to trace Sanford and I fi-nally found out—he owed me over $5,000 —finally I found out what he'd done—he'd bailed out of a window in a hotel in Balti-more. So that was the end of him. He must have owed a lot of people. So then after about two years we went into Carnegie Hall and we had studios there and it was a great big place. It was a live-in studio, which few people realize. Of course we had to have an organ, we had a Steinway grand, we had a full recording outfit. Fifty-five pupils a week. But we all went broke because every-body started to owe us money.

We were the last live act to play at Dempsey's on Broadway, Loretta and I. She played the organ and I played the piano. The reason they closed us out, it was a good job, it was from 10 till about 2 o'clock, but it paid us about $400 a week, which was good money at the time, and our agent named Sullivan didn't know what he was doing, so he had us take all our books apart and put blues tunes in which they didn't want. Jack Dempsey was never there; he had only syndicated his name, and they all came in to see Dempsey, and when he wasn't there, well, that's what made them close it up. But that was a good job.

So then after a while we didn't know what to do. We were hard-pressed for money. I finally went bankrupt after the trouble I had in Carnegie Hall. Along about October of 1959 we didn't know what to do because Loretta couldn't get a job here on piano organs. So I happened to think of a fellow by the name of Williams who was an old bandleader that I knew, and he was in Chicago, so I phoned him. And he says, does Loretta play Hammond, and I says, the hell she doesn't. He says, well God al-mighty, get her over here as quick as you can. In Illinois and Indiana sometimes they'll have as high as two organists in the same block.

She opened in Rock Island on Labor Day

in 1959 and that was the last time I saw her. It was simply a business separation because I couldn't make money out there. I have to be in a place where shows originate, and she couldn't make money out here as hard as we tried to get her jobs. She's now an organist in a club in Peoria and she was very very fine. We were married for 16 years, we had no trouble at all. We had a cashbox; whoever needed $10 gets in the cashbox and didn't have to ask the other guy. If we had to spend money like on a refrigerator, then we'd consult each other, but that is the way I like to work. The money is there, if you need it, go get it, and no questions asked, because if you can't trust the other guy, what the hell can you expect.

So that's the kind of a person I'm looking for at the present time. I get a letter, oh, about once a year. She knows all my troubles. She also belongs to 802; she never did give up her membership there. I don't know if she's remarried and I wouldn't ask. It's just one of those things. It was simply the fact that she had to go out there or otherwise we would have been in even worse shape. We never got a divorce, we're just separated, but we're separated long enough now. I asked my attorney and he said it would cost $1,000 to make it formal, but I can't see it unless I wanted to get married again.

But I think she was one of the finest musicians that I've ever run up against in my life. That's saying a lot. She barnstormed for about two years and broke even because I used to fill out her income tax. She had problems of costumes, she had to have eight costumes a week because, you know, playing an organ, you sweat them out, you know. She even went up to South Dakota, she had a hell of a time, and she broke even. After that, she started filling out her own forms so I don't know what happened to her income as far as that's concerned.

That's the story of my three wives. I don't believe in getting married, I believe in having somebody to go steady with, that's all. Because at the present time, no doubt about it, as far as my accident was concerned, it was tough to take, but I came out of it $3,000 more than I asked my attorney to get. So really, I don't have to work for the rest of my life. But I've got prospects. In other words, I could break even with a little to spare with the interest on the money, if I handle it carefully, but I'm not that kind of a guy. That's why I want the Piano Phil's Ramblers.

When I was 16 years old, and I was still in those little short bloomers they wore when I was a kid, we lived in Columbus, Ohio, about a block from an amusement park. I was still about a junior in high school. Charlie Miles ran the place and in order to get into the entertainment business I was willing to do anything. I'd cook hamburgers, I'd work in the slot machines, I'd work in the check rooms. And this particular day they had fourth-grade vaudeville, lousiest vaudeville you ever saw, but it was a summer theater.

I was out nipping tickets on Monday, and I was there about 1 o'clock, taking tickets at the door and Charlie came up, and here I was, a kid in bloomers, and he says, your folks told me you play the piano. I said, yes. He says, well, you're going to have to go down and play the show. Well, when I got through running to the bathroom, you know, I was scared as hell, but I went down there and I never got such a lesson in my life. The pianist was drunk, so I had a chance to play the show. I never played one before but I was a big shot.

You should have seen the manuscript they had — it was all written in four sharps which was an impossible key. It had looked like somebody had walked on it after they had been on the road for 48 days. No chord markings, just a suggestion of a melody, but they were the lousiest keys in the world for sharps.

So I went down there and the first guy says the cue is, locked in the stable with the sheep, which of course was Rocked in the Cradle of the Deep. So he gave me the cue and I played the introduction, then I stopped. He says, what did you stop for? I said, like a big shot, I didn't think you wanted to take it. He says, now listen, let me give you some advice: never stop until the artist stops you. That was one of the best things I ever learned. So I says, what are you going to play it on? He says, now listen, you stop asking questions and play the introduction. So I played the introduction and you know what happened? The cane that he had was a slide trombone and he played it on that.

So I learned about vaudeville fundamentally in one of those theaters. Now as far as the training is concerned, that's the trouble today. I played burlesque for two years; it was one of the finest training grounds, and so was vaudeville. But in Toledo, Ohio, a fellow by the name of Gus Sun had his own circuit, he had fourth-, third-, second- and first-grade vaudeville, and after first grade, then you could go into Orpheum. Later I played Orpheum in Ohio, I played under a fellow by the name of McArdle in an orchestra. But Gus Sun had the finest training I've ever seen because you had to be lousy not to make fourth grade, which is the stuff they had in the amusement parks. Then he would graduate you up the line and after first you could audition and go on to the Orpheum.

As far as the musical background is concerned, I met W. C. Handy a long time ago when he was with a circus for Ringling Bros. He came into town with a 30-piece band, jazz band, swing and did the Mem-

phis blues and all those and I met him at that time. So that's why I know fundamentally the style of Handy. But these guys down at the Jazz Museum and the members of my orchestra keep saying they want to play modern jazz, and I says, no, there's nothing like it. We can play fundamental stuff. I used to use ragtime all the time and I did songs at the piano.

I was in the First World War, I trained at Fort Sheridan just outside of Chicago. I was ready to go overseas, then they transferred me, they graduated me from infantry, but then they sent me to Camp Zachary Taylor, but I had an interesting experience in Chicago because that was when the old Morrison Hotel was up there and we'd meet all those good musicians. Just to make a long story short, there was a show in town called *Oh, Look!* that had the Dolly Sisters and Fox, and at that time I happened to know one of the girls in the cast. It had Billy Van, one of the old comedians. He was really old. But the Dolly Sisters came out to Fort Sheridan and they asked me to play for them, and these were the real ones, and I met them and Diamond Jim Brady.

So when the show was out there, and they had big stage shows, probably 1,000 in the audience, they liked the playing so well that every time they went out on a nonpaying date, they'd get the general to let me go along with them. Harry Fox used to do "I'm Always Chasing Rainbows," and I can give an exact imitation of the way that he used to do it. There was a girl by the name of Pat, she was in the Capitol Ballet in New York, and later when I was playing burlesque in San Francisco about 1942, who came together but Pat and Bill. He was a comic and Pat was the one that used to put the dances together. Just shows you how, after many years, you meet people who've been in the business.

In 1927 I went over to Paris and I

caught Josephine Baker in the Follies-Bergère. It was a wonderful show, very ornate compared with the Ziegfeld Follies. There was a fellow by the name of Bill Thompson and I met him in 1927. Now about 1953, I played out here for the Kingsbridge Hospital with a girl by the name of Sally Burke and we had stars on there. We had Morey Amsterdam that I played for and many others. But we were out there rehearsing early one night, and I saw this fellow Bill Thompson, and I says, it seems to me I know you. He says, yes, and we got together, and you know that we'd met each other at the Follies-Bergère in 1927. That shows you how it is in show business.

As far as the Follies were concerned, I got a good story there, because I saw all the Follies from 1914, 1915. A friend of mine named Stan Jay who later was a captain in the Indian Army, he had a five-minute spot. I knew the rest of them, Ed Wynn. No, I didn't go with any of the Ziegfeld girls; they were too expensive. I knew them, but. . . . Fanny Brice was fine. There was a fellow by the name of Bob who went with one of the girls from the Follies.

But I met Ed Wynn, he was at Ohio State University once during Assembly Hour and we said, how do you manage to get all these jokes of yours. He said he had a file of over a million jokes. He said that there are only eleven original jokes. One of them is, of course, who was that lady I saw you out with last night? That was no lady, that was my wife. So then he paraphrased it, and he'd say, who was that ladle I saw you out with last night? That was no ladle, that was my knife. And he kept associating them like that, and if you wanted a joke about anything, he could give it to you. He wrote his material himself. But there was one joke that I used to use; I took it after that, and I used to use this for a while.

Someone would say, who was that lady I saw you out with last night? And I'd say, that was no lady, that was my brother, and besides, he has a problem. But I knew Eugene and Willie Howard and all the rest of them. I think Ed Wynn was probably the best actor I've ever seen in my life. His timing was so superb.

When I came back from India in 1933, I went to Elliott Nugent and he said, you've got something here that's probably worth about $25,000 or $30,000 — which was a lot of money in those days, for this musical I had written. So the music was acceptable. A fellow by the name of Nat Hawkins, famous conductor, he liked the music very much and the score. So he turned me over to Jack Lazarus, who was the editor, but they can always find an excuse why they don't take something. Now in this case, it was simply that it might be an international situation. The musical was called *Ming Hoy,* which I had written while I was in the Far East.

There was something very interesting about this story. Nat Feinstein was the musical director and he loved the score and he wanted me to stay with Paramount to be a musical advisor, do scoring and write music out there. It was a wonderful chance. I didn't do it because there was a bad boy of music, a fellow by the name of Boris Morros. Nat left to conduct symphonies and I was with Boris Morros for about a week. Incidentally, Boris Morros turned out to be a vice president of Paramount and he bankrupted Paramount. But then the story came out later that what he was doing was counter-espionage work for the U. S. Government. But I didn't like him so I went back to San Francisco. That's where I made a fundamental mistake. Decidedly, I should have stayed at Paramount.

Actually, with Elliott's help, I was on two pictures out at Paramount. It was a hell of a job out there because central casting had 15,000 people. So they had a show out there called *Lives of a Bengal Lancer*. Well, I was just back from India, I rode a horse and I had done big-game hunting so I went down one morning. Elliott called some guy up and said I could be a technical advisor for them which would have suited me fine. I went down and the guy was hot as the mischief for me, says, come back after lunch and sign the contract. And I went back, and the guy didn't even know I had been in the office in the morning. God knows, that's the way it goes in Hollywood. Somebody probably gave him something under the table in the meantime.

But actually, there was one picture that I was in called *She Loves Me Not*. Bing Crosby, Miriam Hopkins, and Kitty Carlisle. Kitty Carlisle, I think she's wonderful. She's still on, you know, on the panel shows. I wasn't actually in the picture, but Elliott wanted me to learn how to make pictures. The second one I was on several years later was with Bob Hope and Dotty Lamour, *My Favorite Brunette*. Again I was learning how to make pictures, but I made contacts with all these wonderful people.

I met Bob Hope. He used to come down to the golf club in the morning. Elliott used to say to him, well, Bob, what are the three lousy jokes you got today? Bob would give him three, so he'd throw them out. Bob's jokes that he wrote were the lousiest things. But I got great experience there being able to see the rushes and all. So if I had stuck closer to Elliott, we'd have been out of trouble.

But show business has been in my blood all my life, I've never done anything else. I'm looking forward to 1974. I want to start with Town Hall concerts and then I want my own show, Piano Phil's on Broadway. I won't be happy until I see my name in lights on Broadway.

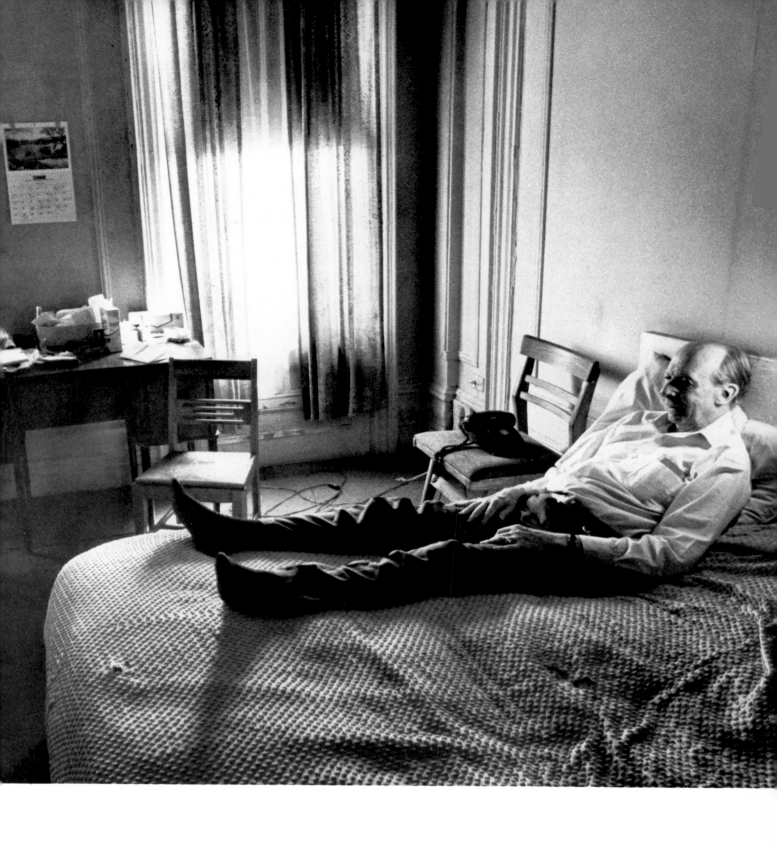

AL GREINER

When I was very young on a farm, I can
remember daydreaming about what Broadway was like because of what I had read
in the newspapers. Then, when I was about
eight years old, I started practicing the

piano, not because anyone made me, but because I liked it. . . . My music education in college ended up in teaching football. But during college I worked my way through school on a radio station playing the piano and when I left college, I went to Minneapolis and got in a group called the Crazy Monte Cristos. In 1933 we shipped down to a radio station in Del Rio, Texas, and from there I organized a six-piece band and played around in different places with a famous group of unicyclists called the Pageant Jewett for one and a half years. We all played the theaters in the Middle West. I played sax in the band.

When I was about 22, the Pageant Jewett group went to Europe, so I became the manager of a vaudeville show with about 40 people in it. We played as far east as Scranton, Pennsylvania, as far south as Jacksonville, Florida, mostly one-night stands. We toured all over and we had some starvation days. It was pretty rough because you were only paid when you worked. You know what the salary was? $4.25 a day. That was low even in those days, but I did it because of my basic love for music. I liked vaudeville. I liked that type of life even though at that time it wasn't at its best anymore. . . . I might have been quite big in it, except for one thing. And that was the fact that I had to play the same music day in and day out and that got awfully tiresome. I think that made me grow away from vaudeville at that time. I just couldn't stand to play the same music all the time.

So after that I took the nucleus of that band and played some of the best ballrooms and so forth in the Middle West and South and colleges. I stayed with that group until I went into the army. But playing with that band, I got to meet other people who were performing around like Al Jolson. To play for him was probably the greatest thrill I've

ever had. We played "Mammy," "Quarter-to-Five," which I've always loved, "Swanee," "Sonny Boy," and so on. He was great; he had a feeling for those songs. I also played for him while I was in the army. He happened to see me as I was walking away from drill in basic training and he remembered me and asked me to play for him again.

Before, in Ohio in 1934, before I had even gotten a band together, I was playing in a nightclub for $17 a week and a fellow came over and asked if I'd like to play a burlesque theater. I was pretty naive then. I don't think I even knew what burlesque was so I said sure, because he offered me $27.50 a week, which I considered a lot of money. They had stripteasers there, but I didn't pay much attention. What I really enjoyed were the comedians on the show like Abbott and Costello.

I go back to this because I want to mention something. While I was there, a man from the National Theatre came over and asked the manager for a young piano player for the show. They took me up to the National Theatre and I was introduced to a young girl, about 11 or 12 years old, who had just broken away from her sisters. Her name was Frances Gumm, and I rehearsed her a little and thought, wow, this girl is something. After the first show she went over to her mother and asked for five cents to buy an ice cream cone. This was coming out of the mouth of a young girl who five minutes before had sung "You Made Me Love You" like a grown-up. That little girl was Judy Garland and today, when people ask me who I consider the greatest performer, not the greatest singer because you've got a lot of them, Sinatra, Sammy Davis, Al Jolson, but I consider Judy Garland the greatest performer of our century.

I was thrilled to death when I saw her in *The Wizard of Oz* in the movies but I never saw her personally again until she played the Palace in the early 1960s. I went backstage and she remembered me. Of course, she was entirely different by then. She had had a rough life and wasn't a young girl anymore. She was pathetic, really. I think MGM might have been partly responsible, making her work when she was tired. A young girl at that age should have some time of her own and a certain amount of rest. I think they made her work too hard because they knew they had a money girl here, and I think they expected too much.

After I got out of the army, I came to New York, finally, to find out what Broadway was like. . . . I met Connie Francis in 1956 and she sang good and played the accordion. I always had a feeling, because of her capabilities and her style, that she would make it, but I didn't know she'd be as big as she was. I remember she had made a couple of records, but nothing had happened and she said, Al, I'm going to go to New York University and study French. I said, Connie, you won't like it. But she said, I'm not getting anywhere here. She'd always come in, though, and sing. We'd play clubs and affairs and I could see it was a big part of her life. She did go to NYU for a time but she didn't stay long because she couldn't get over the fact that she wanted a hit record. And she made it.

Things had been pretty quiet for me in the last few years until last August 1972, when Edna Thayer, who I've known off and on over the years, came to me and asked me to play an audition for her at the Automat on 46th Street. There was no microphone, an old piano that had seen its best days, but I did it. In the meantime, some photographers came from the *Village Voice* to take our pictures performing at the Automat, but I didn't think anything of it. The following week, one of my students said my picture was in the *Village Voice* with an article.

Two weeks later *The New York Times* had a big picture of Edna and myself with an article, which really started the ball rolling. A few weeks after that, Eyewitness News, NBC News, I think all the channels, came over to see us. I really didn't think it would last, but we're still going strong after six months.

On Tuesdays, we perform at the Automat on 86th Street and Wednesdays and Thursdays, we're on 46th Street. I also teach quite a few youngsters and I have some good talent. But it's hard because years ago, these kids had outlets and exposure for their talent. . . . When you work with young people, they keep your spirits up, they give you a very uplifting outlook on life. I suppose the fact that I lost the sight of one eye has also given me a different philosophy on life. I'm interested in making people happy and when you see some young talent like Connie Francis, it gives you a certain amount of satisfaction to know you're helping them do something they like to do.

I wouldn't change my life one bit. I'd do all the same things over again. I've had a lot of help through the years. In 1958 I wrote a Christmas song, "God Bless Santa Claus," which has become kind of a standard now. . . .

I've had good times and some bad ones. Back in 1953, I had hemorrhaging ulcers and almost didn't make it. There are eleven days out of my life that I can't account for. Then in 1962, I had a detached retina and had three operations. I was a pretty unhappy boy when I realized I was losing sight in my left eye. But there's something in me, as probably in most people, that keeps me from feeling sorry for myself. Keeping busy also helps. I enjoy helping young people. There's nothing wrong with them that a little help won't cure. They make life worthwhile.

70

EDNA THAYER

Meet me at the Automat
Meet me at the Automat,
Any old time, I know.
Meet me at the Automat
I'll be there you know.
The food is simply delicious
Ice cream and the donuts, too.
So meet me at the Automat
And I'll autograph my name to you.
Edna Thayer — the Automat Girl.

I'm Edna Thayer.
I'm known as the Automat Girl. I've been in vaudeville since I was three years old, and I'm now 65. I'm also known as the Cafeteria Canary and the Jenny Lind of the steam tables.

I've been in show business for 62 years, I started when I was three years old. My mother and father were staying in Canada and they had two Scotch girls on the bill who wore kilts. The color of the kilts took

my eye, so I called my mother over and I said, Mama, I can dance like those girls and make money for you. So she made me a little Scotch outfit and I sang and did a Scotch dance. You know how you hold your hand in the air in that kind of dance? Well, I used to get tired of holding my hand up and I used to put it on top of my head.

My mother and father did a vaudeville act called The Thayers, featuring Baby Edna. I was Baby Edna. My mother sang and danced and did talk, and my father played the violin and did comedy. We played the Keith Orpheum circuit, the Loew's and all that.

I remember when I was five, and we were playing on this show in vaudeville, a man came to my parents and said he liked their act and that they would get a postcard from him later. Well, they did, and the card said they were to come to rehearsal for a tab show in New England. A tab show is a small show, about 15 people. So my parents went to the show and my father was such a good manager that he managed all five shows there at the same time. Then they gradually increased the show until they had one big production and it used to play with Eddie Cantor. I was on that show and I used to do numbers like "Mammy's Little Coal-Black Rose" in blackface. They used cork on my face and I played a little black boy.

Then when I was 16 years old during the Depression, my parents were having a hard time so my mother took me into an empty theater in Chicago to do an audition for the manager of a burlesque show and they hired me to be the soubrette of the show. I was in that show for six months and they used to tease me and call me "the kid." They were very nice people, very homelike people. They used to ask, where's the kid, brushing her shoes again with the curtain? I used to do that. I also used to draw pic-

tures on the wall of the dressing room and I'd color them with all the makeup and they'd scold me for that, for marking up the walls. I did 13 scenes and I sang about eight numbers and did tap dancing. And in the burlesque house I sang, "I Wonder What's Become of Sally," dressed like a little newsboy. I was only 95 pounds at the time and wore a size 8 shirt and pants, and I used to tear the house down with that number. It was a ballad with a dramatic recitation in it. I wrote the recitation myself. Here's how it went:

She was the queen of our alley
Gee, I loved her so,
She was me very own Sally
Oh, why did she go?
I remember the days gone by
When she and me was pals.
She wouldn't look at another guy
And I was the same with the gals.
But one day she got a chance
With some other feller
To go on the stage and dance,
But the guy was yeller

So with tears in me eyes
I begged her to stay
But she bid me good-bye and went away.
'Twasn't long 'fore I heard
The guy had run away.
If I could lay me hands on that boy
I'd surely make him pay
'Cause she's all I had to love, you see
And now I'm sad at heart,
'Cause she was the only gal for me
And yet we had to part.
No matter what she is
Wherever she may be,
If no one wants her now
Please send her back to me.
I'll always welcome back
My Sally, that old gal of mine.

I did that in a real show, a burlesque show, where they did stripteasing and everything and I used to tear the house down with it.

Once we landed in New Orleans with 20 cents in our pockets during the Depression but we had a job to go to, so my mother's old boss, Mr. Marcus who had the tab shows, sent my mother $250 after she wired him, and we came to New Orleans. The first day I opened in New Orleans, I did the Sally number with the newsboy outfit. I tore the house down because nothing could follow me. They loved that song.

I've also been writing ever since I was a little girl. The first poem I ever wrote was to my mother. I put a valentine with a bird on it and the bird was crooked on the paper, but I said, Roses are red, Violets are blue, I love my Mommy, and she loves me, too. . . .

I've had success and also some hard times. Once in Chicago during the Depression, I decided to sell balloons in Soldier's Field for a game. I was young and I was cute-looking then, only 95 pounds, and all the boys were buying balloons from me. I had two pockets in my apron and they were bulging out with money, and wouldn't you know, someone picked my pocket and I didn't make a dime.

I've been ill many times but I've always come back. I always look for tomorrow. Tomorrow's another day. I think I was born with a sunny disposition, I guess that's what it is. I'm easygoing and never get angry. I like my fellowman. I've never been jealous of other people.

I hadn't written much at that time. I only started writing songs about 25 years ago. I was sitting in a room after having been operated on, and I was feeling blue, so my mother says, Edna, why don't you write a song. I said, Mama, how can I write a song, where am I going to get the music? She said I'd find a way, and so I went around humming and that night I said, Mama, I wrote a song and put your name in it and it's called "Montana May." Later I took it to a publisher, and the first publisher I took it to bought it.

The second time was a little harder. I had been going to this publisher, Bob Miller, for about a year trying to get him to hear my songs, but he would never listen to me. Finally, this one day he said he would hear me but I didn't have my music with me. So he said for me to come back the next day and I did, and he heard my song. He said he had had no idea I was such a good writer. He thought I was one of these amateurs running around. But he said I didn't have anything he wanted then but that he would be interested sometime if I had a song he wanted. So I got out in the hallway and started singing in my head — "Sometime."

Sometime soon, I'll come riding home to
    you,
Till I do, I know that you'll be true.
Sometime soon, we'll have a happy honeymoon

Sometime in the month of June.
Though I'm riding away for the roundup
    today,
I promise that I'll come back soon.
Along the lonely trail,
Somehow I'm never blue,
For I know sometime soon
I'll come riding home to you.

I went back up the elevator and even though I didn't have it on paper or anything, I sang it to him and he took that song and gave me a contract. It took me about five minutes. That's all it takes me to write a song.

I write mostly happy songs, but I wrote one song called "I Give You My Heart" which is a little sad. It's pretty, though. It goes like this:

Sweetheart, you must sail away
A duty which you must obey
But before you go, dear,
Here's what I want to say.
I give you my heart
Guard it tenderly
I give you my heart
Please keep it for me.
I give you my heart
Filled with love all for you.

I can't read a note of music or play an instrument. I just compose the words and music, and sing them to myself in my brain over a few times till I learn them by heart. Then I sing them to an arranger and he puts the notes on them. It's a gift from God, I guess.

I also write a lot of funny songs like "The Funny Little Fish in the Fishbowl." That goes like this:

Oh, the funny little fish in the fishbowl,
Does he ever fall in love?
Oh, the funny little fish in the fishbowl,

What is he thinking of?
Does he ever long like you and me
To have a little privacy?
You think he'll ever reach a goal,
The funny little fish in the funny fish-
    bowl?

I was in vaudeville when vaudeville was starting to go out and once I was in Albany, New York, playing with a big review and we had about three people in the audience. So they closed the theater and we got stranded. The manager made arrangements with Bickford's to feed us and he would get the money later in the week. Well, everyone went to Bickford's and all we did was eat all week long to collect our salary. Then I started working in nightclubs. Do you want to hear some one-line jokes we had in vaudeville? One was — Why does the lady cross the street? Because the lights change. Another was, When is a chicken not a chicken? When she's an old hen. Those were funny then.

I think vaudeville could be revived again. The teen-agers would love it. I could tell last night, they sat enthralled at the Big Band show. The only trouble is, there's no place to train them anymore. They used to have variety, prima donnas, jugglers, magicians, dancers, they had everything. But now it's all rock and roll; the same groups do the same thing.

They used to have amateur nights; all the amateurs would try out and if they were good, they'd get applause, but if they weren't good, they'd get the hook. They would just grab you by the collar and pull you off the stage, and the audience would throw tomatoes and eggs at you if they didn't like you. But that never happened to me. I never did an amateur night. I was a professional from the time I was three years old.

I've been doing all right in the past few

77

years, too. Once I went in to see Johnny Carson and they told me, sorry, Johnny's in conference, so I walked out in the hall. I walked down towards the elevator, and all of a sudden a voice said, Miss Thayer, Miss Thayer. I turned around and it was Andy Smith, a writer. He asked me if I still did a lesson in personality—that's a thing I do with all the imitations—and I said yes. He said, then we want you on the show, and that's how I got on Johnny Carson's show. That was in 1968. . . .

My favorite song is "There's Always Tomorrow," and that's my philosophy.

There's always tomorrow
To look forward to.
There's always tomorrow
To start life anew.
So let's live this moment
Of sweet ecstasy,
I treasure the love, dear,
That you give to me.
Let's think of the future,
Remember the past.
Remember, darling,
True love will last.
There's always tomorrow,
So let there come what may.
We'll live this moment
We have today.

I've lived in the Times Square area for 37 years, but, oh, how it's changed. It used to be so wonderful. You see, at night when people would go to the movies or the theater, they would dress up in evening clothes and look beautiful. Now they go in slacks or any old way at all, hippies. It's become tawdry. The element has changed, the class of people.

I started working here at the Automat in July 1972. It came about this way. I was sitting in my chair at the Automat eating my dinner when my friend said the presi-

dent of the Automat was in the building by the vegetable stand. My friend said to go, so I went and I saw the man and I said, I wrote an Automat song, would you like to hear it? And he said, yes, so I sang it softly for him. He told me to come to the office on Monday. He listened to my other songs and he thought they were great, so I said, why don't you let me sing them at the Automat?

He thought that was a great idea, so he put a piano in and the first night there were a handful of people, there was no microphone, and I sang all alone. Gradually, though, my friends came and they all wanted my job, so I had to put them to work. Now we have about eight acts, Al Greiner plays the piano, and we have a good show. We have fans that stand outside the window knee-deep and they wave and smile and they're all happy. I try to bring a little happiness and joy to people. I've always wanted to make people laugh. That's my ambition.

There are a lot of old performers who come in here, and there's one lady, she's 82 years old—Lillian Ashton—who has known me since I was three years old. She worked for my parents in vaudeville, and when I was very sick and down and had lost my parents, she came every day to the hospital to see me. She brought me food and things that I needed. She was wonderful to me. She still comes in and listens to me sing the "Automat Song."

Oh, you'll always find them at the Automat,
A boy and a girl each day.
Though he hasn't much money
When he's with his honey,
Everything's okay.
With a hand full of nickels
And a heart full of love,
He carries trays in a day

80

She's always dreaming of.
He buys her this and that
And they sit and chat
And plan a future bright,
Oh, you'll always find them at the Automat,
Where boy meets girl each night.

Here's another favorite of mine.

Don't dunk a donut
If you don't know how to dunk,
Cuz a donut ain't a donut
If you don't dunk a hunk.
Dunk it in your coffee
Or milk or in your tea.
If you don't dunk a hunk.
It's simply delicious,
I know you will agree.
But don't dunk a donut
If you're dining at the Ritz.
If you dunk a donut there,
The headwaiter will have fits.
He'll bellow to the floor
And then show you to the door.
So don't dunk a donut
If you don't know how to dunk.
Cuz a donut ain't a donut
If you don't dunk a hunk.

I really wish vaudeville would come back. I think it could, too. They had the big bands years ago, and they've brought them back. I saw it last night, Frankie Liston, and the show was great. They had pictures on each side of the stage blown up of all the band leaders that are gone now, but their music is still living on. And being a songwriter, I hope my music will live on, too.

Oh, we all grow old someday
No matter what we say.
When we lose our pep
And we're out of step

And our hair starts turning gray.

When there's peace in the world once more,
There'll be a happy day in store.
There'll be a world's holiday, and people will say,
At last God has had his way.
When there's peace once more in the world,
There'll be such joy for every boy and girl.
The bells will be ringing
And the birds will be singing
And freedom's flag will be unfurled.
When our boys come home to stay
We will have a world's holiday.

EMMA HYMAN

Worked 35 years I did. I went all through. I worked in the Ziegfeld Follies in 1915. I juggled, I can't juggle anymore. I worked with my husband, man and wife. He used to balance me on the bridge of his nose on a chair, like I'm sitting on now, with the back across his nose and me sitting and the four legs on the chair turned upside down on his nose. It was one of the many tricks. I met my husband in London. He was working an organ out on the street and I was dancing out on the street. It is a long story. It started in 1908.

I went through Ziegfeld Follies and he put a show on and I was in the chorus, one of the showgirls, and we used to walk around smothered in balloons and as we walked by they used to pop the balloons. Diamond Jim Brady was there and when we walked by he used to bust the balloons — pop–pop–pop. . . .

I had the command performance to show before the queen of England in Buckingham Palace, London. When he went to balance me on his nose, the queen came up and said — what is he going to do with her now? He didn't take a bit of notice of her — he went right on balancing me. I was

there on his nose. I sat on four legs on a chair and tilted back on the chair across his nose. That was show business.

Mr. Hyman was very very good — sick 10 years — I like to juggle and dance. I don't like to talk anymore since I'm so old. What is left for me — the bitter end.

We used to have choruses. I used to dance and sing — you know the American Theater — used to sing:

My moonlight girl
My midnight girl
I love you

I was married and divorced and married. This was a clever man, he had a mark on the bridge of his nose. We had a beautiful act. He was a good-looking man but he loved the ladies. He loved the ladies too much for me. They would come to the stage door and ask for him. Ask for Mr. Gasgoid, that was his name.

I worked on the bill with Charlie Chaplin. He played a number called "A Night in an English Music Hall" and he used to play and juggle and fall out of a box onto the stage.

I am a has-been. My husband got killed. He was out in Frisco and he had been drinking and he crossed the road when he shouldn't have. A car came and hit him and knocked his brains out. That's what happened to my husband. We did a beautiful act together.

HARRY KADISON

How long have I been in show business? Most of my life, I guess, most the past 30 years, 35 years. Harry Kadison, like Madison but with a K. I'm living in Times Square for the last 20 years, but I've been here practically all my life because this was show business — this was the center of show business. I began in 1925 when I was a kid. But then I left it and came back to it, and left it and came back to it.

I've had some good parts, I've had some bad parts. I've had 25 Broadway flops in a row. I mean what else can I say to you. I've been in burlesque, I worked in burlesque, I worked in vaudeville, I'm the one that killed vaudeville, now you know why it's dead. I came in and they killed it, they closed it, they did away with it. I stage-managed vaudeville units, I've been on Broadway, Broadway shows, been in the movies, been on television. I've been on the radio.

Well what is to tell, it was a wonderful thing, it was nice, it was a grind, but it was very enjoyable 'cause you worked with wonderful people and you had a lot of laughs and the funniest part of it is — burlesque you have — is a wonderful way of life. You have a lot of fun — I just don't mean for sex, I just don't mean for women, I mean its — in those days well sex — er burlesque was a wonderful thing and I think I have learned more from working in burlesque about acting than I've ever learned in all the time I've been on the Broadway stage. Well, there were things you learned in burlesque that you can't learn on the Broadway stage as you learned in vaudeville. I used to learn timing in vaudeville and in burlesque.

Bob Frier once had a discussion with me. I met him one time having a hot dog and he was talking to me and he says Neil Simon — fella who wrote *Odd Couple, Plaza Suite* — says that actors don't have timing. And I told him to go back and tell Neil Simon that the actors he hires have no timing. If he hires burlesque performers, he'd have no problem with timing. Well, timing is an intangible thing — you've got to have it or you don't have it. You either learn it or you don't learn it. The average person doesn't know what it is, but for an actor and a director and a performer, it's a most valuable thing. By working, by facing the audience, by working, the only way you can learn it is by working.

See, in burlesque we used to do four shows a day, five shows on Saturdays, seven days a week. In vaudeville you used to do four shows a day, seven days a week. The same thing, and that's when you learn it. And you'll find in vaudeville and burlesque that you can't tell the audience where to laugh — they'll laugh when they want to. One time they'll laugh in this spot, the next time they won't laugh here, they'll laugh there. Who are you to tell them when to laugh? They paid their money; they're going to laugh when they want. And there's where your timing comes in. You have to be prepared for when they laugh, not when you want them to laugh.

Now there's where burlesque comes in. You go out in burlesque and you do a skit, and all of a sudden the audience throws the answers at you. So the comic goes into a different skit and you've got to go follow it. You see? In other words, you're on your own, rather than having a set of lines that you got to deliver every week, every day, every night. And that's where you learn. And the only way you can learn is by working and where can an actor work today. There's no work. An actor, he lays off for three or five years and then you expect him to come up and do a beautiful job. Now you take a plumber. Let him lay off for five years, stay away from his trade for five years. When he comes back, he won't be as good as he was, will he? It'll take him a little while to come in again.

Well, it's the same thing. Acting is more elusive, yet, it's the simplest thing in the world. Why is it the simplest thing in the world? Well, there's a saying in the theater. Never do a scene with a child or an animal. They'll always steal the scene. You've heard that. Well, discount the animal; they're not human. They don't say any particular child, they say *any* child. Which means you as a child were a great actress.

What happens as you grow up? Why don't you have it? You still have it, but society taught you not to use it. Have you ever heard a mother tell a child — don't talk with your hands? And what happens when the girl — the child — the boy or the girl is 12 or 13 years old? They send them to ballet school to learn what to use what they told them not to use. And what nature meant them to use.

What is the first thing a child talks with? His hands. So why do you restrain it? Who screams louder than a child? The minute he's born, he's yelling at the top of his voice, right? Why doesn't he get laryngitis or a sore throat. That same child when he grows up, the minute he yells — laryngitis or a sore throat.

So naturally when a child grows up, they get on stage they don't know what to do. But a child — never have to tell him what to do with his hands on stage — he knows it. How many times they tell him — don't daydream — right? You're stifling your imagination. Can you tell me any little girl playing with her doll that you can't convince that girl that that doll is not her daughter? But when you tell her not to do it, you're stifling the imagination. Yet when they can have a man that's great, an executive, he has executive power, he has personality, he has executive ability, he has imagination. So why do you stifle it in a child.

We haven't created a great actor since Barrymore, and we never will. 'Cause we don't have teachers that teach them these things. Take your breathing, for instance. Well, watch people how they breathe when they're standing, but when they're sleeping they won't breathe that way. They won't breathe that way when they're sleeping. And when they're sleeping is the proper way to breathe. Take a one-minute-old baby — he's breathing properly. I'm just showing you why. Someone told me they're going to a voice teacher where the teacher's going to teach them how to breathe diaphragmatically. I say run away from him because he cannot teach you something you were born to do. And you were born to breathe diaphragmatically — what is he going to teach you? How can he teach you something that you were born to do? . . .

They used to come here, vaudevillians, old performers that used to retire, used to come here to the Automat, here on 47th and Broadway, 46th and 47th to meet people. Today they come in once in a while every summer and I meet them — they ask me where everyone is and I say — they're no longer here. They say — nobody is here? And I say no. For the first place, the Automat people have chased them out. Yes. They don't want them to sit around. Ask them why, don't ask me. Whereas before, this was the meeting place, either here in the Automat or in front of the Palace Theatre. If we sit here long enough, he'll come over and tell us to move. And so, they don't come here anymore because there's nobody to see. Whereas one time, anytime you wanted to meet somebody, as I've said before, you'd either — in front of the Palace Theatre or the Automat. This was the meeting place of all vaudevillians. They don't — there is no more vaudeville. There's no place to meet, there's no more vaudeville. They used to have the NVA Club; that's no longer in existence. National Variety Artists Club. No, because there's no vaudeville. There's no vaudeville anymore left. There's no vaudeville around.

I'm living, but I'm not active in vaudeville. So everybody moved to where they want to live. I'm a New Yorker, so I'm living in New York. Others went to Florida, others went to Chicago, others went to — wherever they had relatives. They left. Wherever their home town was. Very simple.

There's nothing here for them — certainly nothing attractive on Times Square. Most of them are working at other jobs. Oh, some of them are retired. Some are in real estate business. Whatever they could get. They got to live. Very few. There's no stage. There's no vaudeville, there's no burlesque, there's no work.

There used to be a time when I'd lay off, I wasn't working in a stage play or anything of that sort. I'd pick up a comic and do a week, a club date, and the club date would pay me my expenses for the week. But now there's not any more club dates even. And — as I spoke to an agent whom I knew very well — I said to him, Eddie, my voice is coming back. I'd like to — I'd like — may I come up to see you? He doesn't say anything — drinking his coffee. I say, Eddie can I use a word — you bastard — I'm talking to you — I'm telling you my voice is coming back — I may come up and ask you for a job this summer. He says, Harry, what can I tell you, how many times do I tell you, all they want there are young kids. Whether they can sing or not or can perform or not, it doesn't matter — they're young. So what are we going to do? So why should they stick around?

And the young breed is different than the old breed. The old breed — you worked in vaudeville, you made a friend — you had friends. Today, here today, gone tomorrow. I can't think of his name — he used to sing in burlesque. Every time he came around looking for me. How are ya, how are ya, let's have coffee. Last year he came around he says, nobody around? I says, no, nobody around. He says, no point in coming around here anymore. I says no, there's no point in coming around. They want to come back and meet their old friends and talk and sit and kibbitz. No place to go and nobody tells me, you can't stop progress. If this is progress, well, I don't know.

TEDDY LESLIE

It doesn't matter what a place is like as long as we know someone is there. Show people stick together. You know about "Hey, Rube," don't you? You could go out into the street and holler "Hey, Rube" and people would come running to help you. We're at home here.

Note:

Teddy Leslie, officially Lorrie Allen, at the Jackson Hotel, 139 West 45th Street, a resident of that hotel for 21 years, died in 1969, after having been moved out of the Jackson Hotel. Teddy preferred to live there and stay in Times Square that was her home. Teddy's last show with her partner, Bobbie, was in the Park-Sheraton. When there was nothing left for burlesque dancers, she and Bobbie became cashiers in movie theaters in the neighborhood. On the bureau is a photo of her former partner, Bobbie, and herself — taken before the bump and grind circuits dried up.

CLEO LEWIS

I was an old show woman years ago. Singing, dancing, acting and contortionist. I would do a running split, but can't do it now. It is one of those things. I guess I'm on the way out. I never bothered anyone. I tried to stay by myself. I guess that is why I'm alone today. So anyhow I have this

apartment and I rent a couple of rooms. I have been in the building 40 years and the way Times Square has changed is brutal. You get mugged in the hallway — you aren't safe nowhere. Times Square used to be beautiful. You could go up the street and you could be happy and you had a lot of friends.

I quit show business in 1966 and took a cashier's job at the Penny Arcade and I was in the booth in 42nd Street, Times Square. A friend came up and said, Gee, Cleo, you look tall. I said, you would too if you were standing up. He said, get a chair for this woman. I was seven years in that booth, and got my Christmas and vacation. So then they switched me to 52nd Street and they didn't give it anymore, and I said, I want my Christmas. I worked all night long till 5 in the morning, no extra money, no nothing. I got mad one day and I said I'm glad you got your money; you can have it, but you are not going to make a slave out of me any longer.

Vaudeville was lovely then. Everyone was your friend then. We had shows every night. I sang good songs and anytime someone would hear a song they would say, Oh, Cleo, I have a song, I want you to sing it. You see, I had a double voice, I did have. I haven't got nothing now. I had a triple voice. I would take a certain song with a key — then I would take it up a high note and then switch it off to a lower note — it's called a double voice.

Down in the Village I knew a lot of people in cabaret. They are all dead now. So this woman wanted me to sing one of her songs. I was the only one that had the verse and chorus. That little punk that just retired, Frank Sinatra, he said that there was no verse to that song. This Georgia — she-he, you know she is AC-DC — she said,

I'd love to have Cleo sing this song. She wrote the song called "My Greenwich Village Sue." She said, I love the way you sing it, so she gave me the copy — the verse and chorus.

So, seeing how he is smart out in Queens, he starts singing the chorus, "My Greenwich Village Sue," but there's nothing to it seeing he didn't know the verse. So my girl friend said, sing the verse. He said, there is no verse. She said, how much do you want to bet there is a verse? My lady friend has the original. She is an entertainer too. He said, oh, you are crazy. She called me up and said, get a cab immediately and come over here, I'm going to put this guy under the table. So when I walked in she said, you don't know this lady but she knows you. Can you play what she tells your piano player? He said, yes, I can follow her, and I said, well, you are going to play the verse of "My Greenwich Village Sue" song.

Frank Sinatra came out and said, who gave you that, and I said, you see this name here, George — Georgette is her female name. He said, oh, she is a dyke. I said, that's right, she wrote the song and the verse and she gave it to me, and there she is right over there, and she was big husky and she said, you want to make something of it? He said, I didn't know there was a verse, and she said, I know because you aren't a real performer. There was a verse and chorus and I wrote it. He never talked to me after that, because I found him out. He was going to tell everyone he wrote the song.

Crazy like this here the old-time performer who used to pick up pennies in cabarets, Tommy Lyon. He is still working around. He is a junkie dope fiend. He sang a song and he said he wrote it. I said, Tommy, you are lying. I'll sing the first verse, the second verse and the chorus to it and you didn't write it. I wouldn't lie about a thing I didn't write. Then I went back in cabaret and I danced and sang. That's why my toes are all cuddled up here. The doctor wants to take that toe off and fix it up. Arthritis got it all turned over the other toe. Can't get shoes. I did tap, toe dancing, acrobatic contortionist and my son was born, he was a contortionist and double-jointed.

I traveled all over the country. I didn't like traveling. It was just a job, a livelihood, just one of those things. Ann and Harry Seymour, you heard of them? I worked with them when we were little kids — Seymour, Claire and Seymour was our act. Claire was my name. Harry was her brother and Anne Seymour is in the pictures now — she plays the old-woman roles of course. We aren't chickens anymore. I was five years understudying Mary Pickford. She got the big money and I done the hard work. I done the rough horseback riding, swimming, acrobats — she didn't do that.

My husband — Mr. Lewis — he was a musician and drummer and he was the first man to have a rack. He had all kinds of monkeys and everything else in there. He worked with them on their toes. My third husband, he was a policeman, 18th Precinct. I outlived all my husbands. They are all gone. This one died from a heart disease while on the police force. This one here was killed in Chicago and the first husband was killed in Chicago by gangsters. I could write a book if I could write. I would write about the poor old me that there was once.

I started show business when I was eight years old. We had 10 shows a day, called a nickelodeon. Five cents you pay to go in. You see four acts and a big moving picture for a nickel. That's why it was called a nickel-odeon — 5¢. That was continuous vaudeville, from eleven o'clock in the morning till eleven o'clock at night. I worked and for years, my mother wouldn't give me a dime, wouldn't give me a penny to go to work. She wouldn't give me anything to eat until I came home at night, and then she would give me a sandwich. I had a tough time. I don't mind. That was in Pittsburgh.

The Seymours came from Pittsburgh, and their father was a booking agent. He had this booking agent and he used to book us in different shows and there was a school act and then it was brought out and I said, I guess we are gone, and he said, no, you are still an act. I'm just following in the idea, and we sang "In Vacation Time, In Vacation Time," so we would sing that like we were taking a vacation from school days. Irving Klause was the school teacher and Charlie Kenan, Anne and Harry Seymour, Ruth Edna, they are the old-timers, Ruth is dead.

We traveled on the road. Mrs. Bitmer, the Seymours' mother, traveled with us. We had to have someone with us. Children weren't allowed in show business unless they had someone older to travel with them. So Mrs. Bitmer traveled with us. I never liked it. I was always a loner. I always wanted to be alone. We would get in a town and all would be grabbing for rooms and I would wait there and sit over at a restaurant and have coffee and chocolate pie until they all got settled in their room and then I would go and get my room all by myself. I didn't want anybody around me. When you are a loner like that, it is better to be alone. I don't like people. Then I got mixed up in cabaret.

I wouldn't go back in show business for anybody. Today show business is crummy, it is vulgar, there is nothing pretty about it.

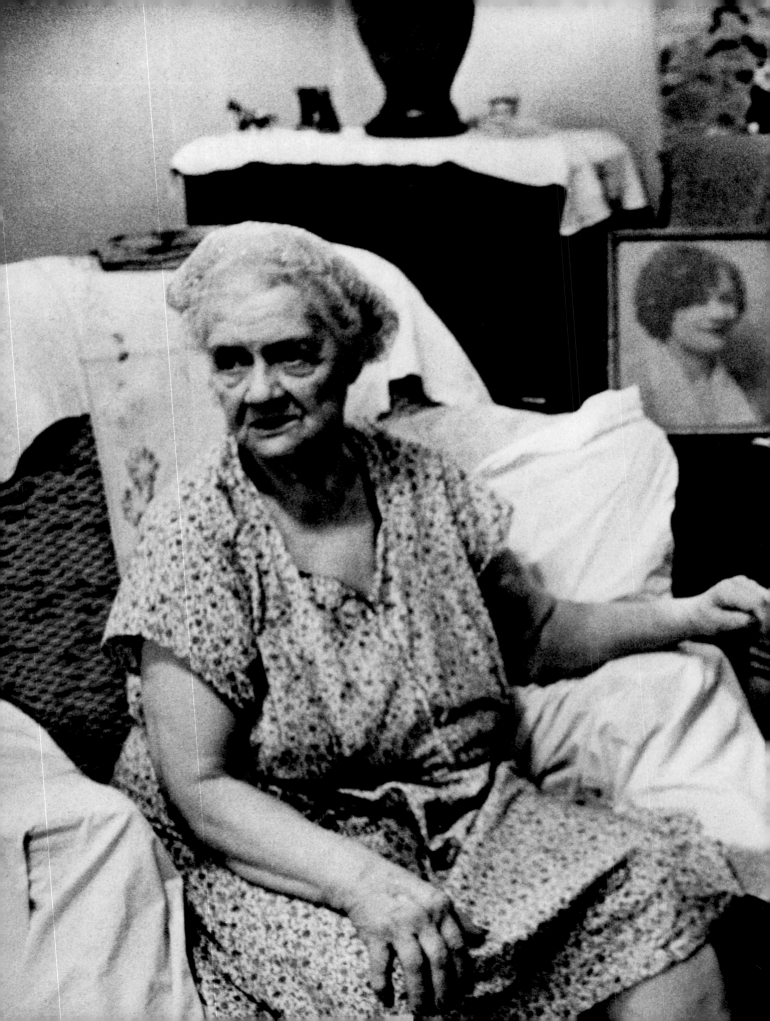

The man across the street was in *Hair*. I said, Stew, don't tell me you are in that show. He said, Cleo, it is the twentieth century!

It is not like your day. I said, I know it is not like my day. I said, I know all about it. A friend of mine was in the dressing room one day and asked her to come in and see the picture and she was ashamed because they got raided on Broadway there. They go to bed with one another naked. I said to her, didn't you like it? No, I did not, she said, and when the police came in, I put my head down and when they put the lights on I went out. It's vulgar, all those dirty shows. Filth, that's what it is.

I worked in a cabaret once and the boss said, Cleo, you have to put on some skin tights. I said, What? He said, you have to put skin tights on and do the devil act. I said, the devil I will. We didn't have vulgarity in my day. We had a lot different shows and went all over America one time. The boss called us in and said, look, now, I'm not saying you can't go with any of these fellows and girls, but if you start out with that man, you stay with him all during the show, not in and out with different men, different women. You are like a man and wife. That is the way we did it in my day. He said, did you get mixed up with anybody? I said, I don't want anybody.

I met my first husband, the Irishman, when I was working a cabaret in Chicago and he was a waiter and he was hanging around me and hanging around me. He didn't ask me, he just took me down and we got married, that's all. He didn't say a word, and then he took me home to his mother and she said, you have to get married in the church. She said, the justice of the peace is not our religion. I said, it is anybody's religion. She said — no, not ours.

He was Catholic. Then he turned out to be a bum and I had to leave him, come on to New York, went in the shows, never bothered him after then.

Then Mr. Lewis was in show business. He had a band and I used to sing in front of the band. I used to work in front of his band. Then he died and I was alone again. Then I had the policeman, he died in '47. So if you kill three of them, you don't take the fourth one, do you? No, I had my share I guess — gray old world.

I have one girl friend yet. There is never a Christmas that we don't call up. Flo Riley — she is a grandmother. She raised her 21 grandchildren. Kay, her daughter, was stuck on my boy. But there is never a Christmas that I don't get a card. She never comes to visit. Her daughter won't allow her down in New York. She is afraid she will get drunk. I don't have any beautiful memories — all it was, was work, work, work. All you did was work. I didn't like show business. I was in it to make a living for my mother and myself and that's how I buckled up and made a living and supported my mother all along. But I never liked it. It's all right for giddy people that flies here and there.

I was made to work in show business. I don't know; that's all I know. I can't think of any songs anymore I used to sing. There was a beautiful number; I can't think of the name of it. It was an old, old number, you wouldn't know it. I can't think of anything. After you get out of show business, you can't think of anything. In fact, when you get old and sick like me, you can't think of anything. You think about dying, getting in the ground somewhere. I want to be cremated. I don't want to live any longer. It is too vulgar, too hard, vulgarity.

Seeing a man and woman lay on the street together, naked, vulgarity personified.

I can't remember songs, the brain doesn't work. A song I loved so much was:

Like a baby needs its mother, dear,
That's how I need you

I used to sing that to my baby. I can't think of it now, but they brought memories, lovely memories.

Sometime when someone needs something,
Someone makes someone blue

Those songs you've never heard, honey, they are old, old numbers. I used to have customers, who would say, Cleo, I just bought two new numbers; I want you to learn them. I would say, all right, I'll have them for you tonight. I'd learn them and sing them. I had a lot of customers and I worked in Greenwich, Connecticut, and all over. They would bring me in the songs for me to learn and sing. They used to love my voice. It used to be good — it was two tones. I used to have a lot of fight, but I don't anymore.

I shot my second husband twice. He was working up at the Campus and I was working down on 39th Street. He was running around with this woman and I told him when I married him if you want someone, leave me, go with her, but don't fool around while you're with me. So anyhow, he goes with this woman and he was up at the Campus. I walked in and I had a .38 gun. He had the band upstairs. He said to me — Gee, that's funny, my wife never argued with me, but he took his foot out, when I went to go to the bathroom, and tripped me. I said, you're not going to get away with that, Mr. Lewis. He said — no, I don't think I am. So I went to the bathroom and I — when I came back

he was in the bar downstairs and he's talking to the bartender. He looked at me and I said, you son of a bitch, and I shot him a half inch from the heart and they took it out of the shoulder blade. Masonically speaking — Do you know what the Masons are? Well, that's how I got out. They stick together. See, the people of the Campus were all Masons. My second husband was a Mason. We were living on 43rd Street and still he wanted to come back, the bum.

Well, I was a bad girl in my day. It ain't what I used to be, it's what I am today. I don't even want music. I never play the radio.

It's not what you used to be, it's what you are today. I used to sing —

Oh I got the rheumatiz
I got the rheumatiz
and when you get as old as me
you'll just know what it is

I sing it yet when I get these pains. I get a pain in my back to where I can hardly walk.

Honey, years ago I wanted to sing all the time, sing on my job, singing, singing, singing.

When your old wedding ring was new
And the dreams that you dreamed came true
I remember with pride
As I stood by your side

Oh, I can't sing anymore

What a wonderful picture
You made as my bride
Now the gold has left your hair
There is all silver there
Things are not like it was
When your old wedding ring was new.

JOE MADDEN

I started in show business in 1904, when I was 12 years old, as a juggler. And I still do it, even though I'm 80 years old now. I'm going to play a date this coming Easter Monday at the Commodore Hotel. It'll be the fourth time I played their Easter party. I don't do the clown act anymore because of my whiskers, so I do a tramp. I used to play Freedomland in 1961 to 1963 as both, three hours as a tramp, three as a clown. I juggle everything, high hats, straw hats, cigar boxes, tennis balls, cannon balls. I can do five at a time, five tennis balls. I learned to juggle by watching W. C. Fields.

I used to play the family time which means three shows a day, continuous. Big time was two a day, reserved seats, like the Palace and the Orpheum circuits. But I worked steady on the family time.

Last January, I started working in Union Square Park in a movie called *Heavy Traffic*. I was playing a bum. We were shooting right across from May's Department Store on Broadway and 14th Street. I told the director of the movie that in 1904, I played over there when it was Keith's Union Square Theater, four shows a day. It was all circus there at the time. I was an assistant juggler with a little clown suit on. I went around the stage and tried to catch the straw hats. I got $1.25 a day plus meals and board. See, the idea was, if I wasn't working, I'd have to go back to school till I was 18 years of age and then go to work in a factory or as an office boy for $3 a week. So I worked steady every day for $1.25, which was better. The theater would open up at 9:30 in the morning and at 10 o'clock, they would start the shows. The shoppers would come in and take up three or four seats with their bundles, but no one would kick because they were only too glad to get the 15 cents admission fee. After 4 o'clock it was a quarter, and at nights it was 35 cents.

Oh, I could tell you lots of stories. Here's one. Once I was working on the family time and we went through Pennsylvania. We got to a theater in Pittsburgh over a New Year's holiday—I think it was 1920 or so. So the manager is giving everyone a Happy New Year and then he put the schedule up for five shows. One little boy, who was working in a kiddie act called the Five Playmates, came over and said, five shows, mister? The manager says, yes. The little boy said, I don't do no five shows. After four shows I'm going back to my hotel. You see, usually you did four shows and if you did five, you usually didn't get paid for it. The boy's mother asked if that was the policy, five shows, but the boy said, my policy is five shows, then I get paid extra for the fifth show. So after the matinee, the manager came back and said he had just phoned New York and New York said everybody does five shows and everybody gets paid for the fifth show. Now, who do you think that little boy was? Milton Berle, that's who. The stage manager said, I have to give that little Jew boy credit, all the acts come on the holidays to do five shows, he was the only one who protested and kicked. I have to give him credit. . . .

What do I think of Times Square? Times Square has gone to hell, in plain American English. I knew Times Square when it was a respectable place. Now it's skid row, in the slums. Mismanagement, that's all I can say.

MORRIS LLOYD & HELEN McARDELL

MORRIS: I started in show business 66 years ago in 1907. I'm 83 years old. In 1907, the most popular type of entertainment happened to be the wooden-shoe buck-and-wing dance that originated in minstrel shows by colored people many years before. . . .

A friend of mine who was a dancer, came off the road. He was in show business, I wasn't, and he saw me dancing once and said, you and I are going to do a vaudeville act. That's how I got in show business and we opened in the nickelodeons. I played the Palace eleven times in six years. My act in

burlesque, we did a lot of singing and dancing, my wife and I—the Dancing Lloyds. In the beginning, before I worked with Helen, I did a wooden shoe act called Lillian Wright, Lloyd and Clayton. That was in 1910. Then from the dancing act, I went to my own straight singing and dancing, like Primrose dancing. I'd do George M. Primrose and all that stuff. Then, in burlesque, I was a straight man for the comics.

HELEN: One time, he was asked to stand in for Rudolph Valentino, he was so handsome.

MORRIS: Later on when Lou Clayton and I split up, he went with Jimmy Durante. That was around 1913. My wife and I've been together since 1915 from the School Day show.

HELEN: You know how long we've been married—57 years. We met while we were working at the Harlem Opera House in New York City. He was with a big girl act and I was with a kid act, you know, like what they used to call what Gus Edwards had. I was with one of those acts. He was with 12 big showgirls and he was the only man dancing in the act and I was with 7 little school kids, we were all about 12 or 13 years old. Then he went his way and I went my way.

And then Herman Timberg came up to the show just to look at Morris. Herman was a big star and he was thinking of putting on this big production, Gus Edwards's School Days, and I just happened to be on the bill. Well, I must have made some kind of impression on him that time, because my act closed and his act closed and he started to go into rehearsal for this production and one of my girl friends who was in the show, she was one of the schoolgirls, she said to come down just to see her and have lunch with her and while I was there, Herman Timberg saw me and wanted to know if I was working and I said no, so he asked if

I'd like to come in the show, and I said yes. So Morris and I were in the show. He played Tommy Tatters and I played Sassy Little.

Morris and I, we sort of, well, we didn't hit it off the bat, you know, we just sort of gradually got to like each other. And we weren't allowed to be seen with each other, because all the kids were small in that show, very young and there was a call put out by the callboard—any boy or girl that was caught staying at the same hotel—you couldn't even sit on the same seat on the train, we used to travel on private cars, you know. And we couldn't sit next to them, we couldn't eat in the same restaurant, we just had to stay away from them because otherwise, the boys and girls would be teaming up and then there would be trouble. But anyway, they used to sneak around, you know. Morris and I started seeing each other after it closed, kept up our friendship. We didn't get married right away. I guess we must have went together maybe a year and nine months or so. Then we decided to get married and I went home to Jersey and pretended I was 18, but I was only 15, and we got married.

But we didn't tell our folks. He lived with his mother and I lived with my mother and we just went around, we had a grand time. And we did this for two years without telling our folks and then we went with a burlesque show and I was expecting my baby, and I had to tell my mother that we had gotten married. By the way, the show closed the 18th of June and my little girl was born the 22nd of July. I did talking, singing and dancing and Morris was a straight man for the comics. And I was pregnant.

Once in Buffalo, the house manager came to our manager and he said, gee, she's got a funny shape to her, is there something wrong with her? Our manager said, oh, no —our manager knew, of course—and he says, oh, no, we call her our little kewpie doll, she's just built that way. And I got away with it. The wardrobe lady knew about it and she didn't want me to show, so I wore this leather belt, it was leather in the front and lace in the back, and this woman would put her knee on my back and pull it tight. It could have hurt me. It could have hurt my beautiful girl, God bless her, but it didn't. She's a professor in college, in Seattle University, now. She's a wonderful, wonderful girl. We're very proud of her. . . .

MORRIS: Here's a picture taken in a burlesque show of me and this guy, the first burlesque show this comedian was ever in. He got $35 in 1918. He died two years ago and you couldn't get him for $6,000. Bert Lahr. This is a picture of him and me in Dayton, Ohio, and my wife took it. He was an outstanding comedian. I know Jimmy Durante since he first started in 1909 when he got $15 a week at Perry's in Coney Island. He played the piano. When he started with Lou Clayton and Eddie Jackson, that's when he started to talk and when, I guess, Clayton and Jackson went, he was well known by then and he carried on. About 12 years ago, Jimmy was in New York, they had an affair taking people back in a nostalgic atmosphere and I wrote him a letter. I didn't want to call or come up, so this is the answer—Dear Morris: So glad to hear from you. Sure brought back memories and so forth. They got to be so big, such a high level, you can't talk to them, so I don't want to go near.

And that brings me back to this guy, my old pal. I used to teach dancing with the reputation I had as the last one to win the wooden-shoe buck-dancing championship. So this guy lived downtown, he asked if I'd teach him a step here and a step there. So

I said yes. This guy was Georgie Burns.

That was in 1908 and 1909 and he was nothing. But I will say one thing. He developed considerably. Give the man credit, comparing him from 1908 to now.

Now to give you an instance, Nat Burns —his right name I think was Nat Bernstein —he lived downtown and he asked my friend and I to come down and see him do a single act in a little theater called the Hippodrome Open Air, 10¢ admission, and we went down and he was so bad, he was sitting with us and he wanted to go on the next show. The manager said, no, here's your music, here's a buck, I can't use you, go home. Now we go to 1921 after we did this big act, a friend of mine, a writer, came to me and said, I want you to work with a girl I'm taking now and coaching her to be like Gracie Deegan. Now, Gracie Deegan was the first woman to be known as a dumb Dora, you know, like a dumb, stupid dame, we called a dumb Dora. He told me he had to have me because he wrote an act and the only one that he thinks can work with her is myself. Okay, so he gave me her address and I went up and when I saw her, I remembered and said, you worked in Charlie Reilly's Irish singing act. She said yes. Well, all she had done in that act was come out at the end of the act and do an Irish jig. That's all she did. Well, this was supposed to be a comedienne? So I said, look, my wife and I have an appointment with a man who has a route of vaudeville theaters as long as my arm. I said, I don't want to take up your time, I am going to see him; if it's okay, I won't be back if there's no necessity.

The next time I see her, we're working Keith's Indianapolis, and I look out and see Burns and a little woman by the name Gracie Allen. And I look at the program and the guy's doing my whole vaudeville act. So when he saw me standing there, he runs over quickly and says, hey, look, Her-

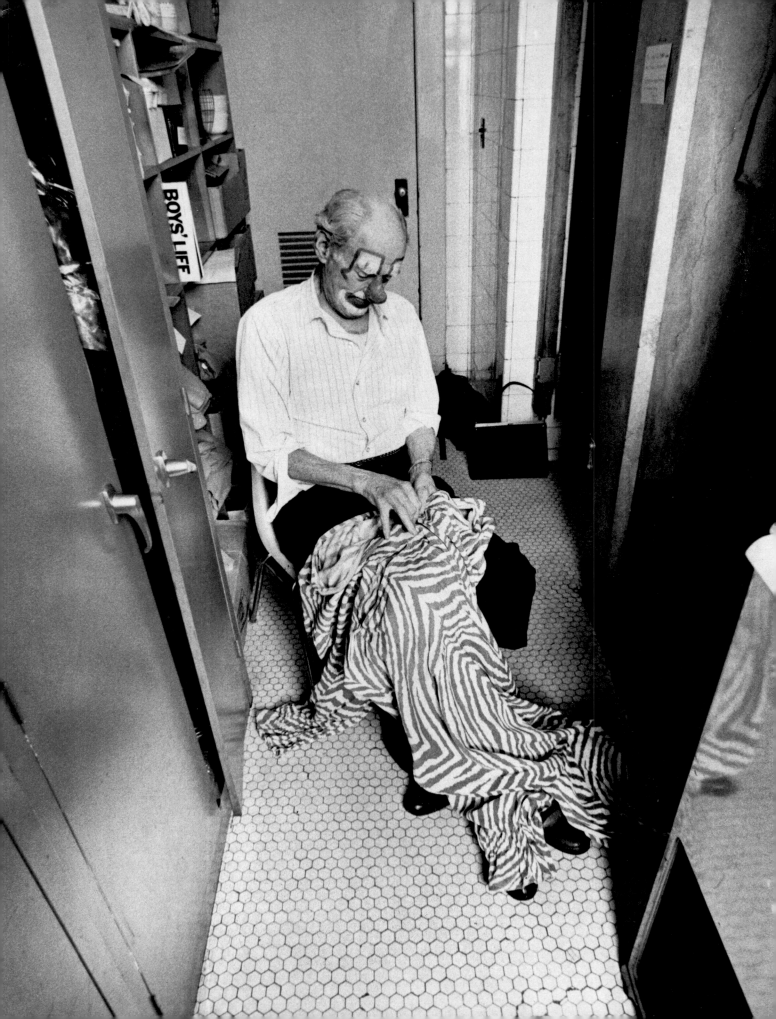

Daily Mirror

NEW YORK 17, N. Y., WEDNESDAY, FEBRUARY 5, 1947 C

BELIEVE IT OR NOT ——By Ripley

THE INDIAN
WENT ON
—A

HELEN McARDLE
"THE STRAWBERRY BLONDE"
New York, N.Y.

M
TOSS
THE W.
GREW 72 POUNDS OF

HAS A REPERTOIRE OF APPROXIMATELY 2500 SONGS
COMMITTED TO MEMORY—AND SINGS ALL BY REQUEST—AVERAGING 125 SONGS NIGHTLY

man Timberg said I could use it and I'm paying him royalty. I said, it don't matter to me. Well, anyway, Burns and Allen went on their way to making a million dollars. Now I don't say, had I said yes and worked with her that we'd be millionaires today. However, I don't know the inside details and connections, but they became millionaires. One word was the cause, the difference between no and yes. Had I said yes, I don't know. There's no guarantee. But I know I said no. So that's my story with Burns and Allen.

HELEN: To make a long story short, he could have worked with Gracie Allen but he turned her down because we were going with another act.

MORRIS: In 1908 there was a place down 14th Street that was the hub of vaudeville. On the program with me was a boy and girl, they were hillbillies and rubes, they were Hogan and West. She later became Mae West. She wanted me to work with her — oh boy, little bit of a girl. Well, in those days, okay, if you had wooden dancing shoes and you said you were a dancer, they let you dance. But she was a poor dancer. She was a kid then. But I said I had a friend of mine, a dancer, who wasn't doing anything, I'll tell him about you. That's how they got the name, Mae West and Frank Wallace, man and wife, and she absolutely denied it for ten years that she was ever married to that man. Why she denied it was a secret I'll never know. Finally she admitted it later. I introduced them. I think they were married for about three years. Later he married another woman and they went and did a ballroom dancing act in nightclubs. But Mae West got a hold of Harry Richman, he was her piano player originally, he made contacts and a friend of mine, Jack Linder, put her out in a show, *Diamond Lil,* and she went up and up.

HELEN: She's a one and only. Nobody like her. Some personality. I never met her but I remember her as a child. I used to go to Loew's Lincoln Square. That's when she was doing her single. She always had such gorgeous gowns and always dressed beautifully. And she wore pants and pajamas in those days before anybody did, she was so far ahead. And she was always beautiful. . . .

After vaudeville died we went into clubs. If we couldn't work together, we would work doing singles. I would go out singing and Morris would go out doing his master of ceremonies and putting on these shows. We would take whatever we could get. I was at the Metropole for 15 years. I was the star of the Metropole. I was called the Strawberry Blonde of the Metropole and I was there singing lots and lots of songs. Then one night, somebody from Ripley's came in — in fact, they came in a couple of nights.

MORRIS: Ripley himself came in. Who else can say that?

HELEN: And they put this in the *Mirror* in 1947. They wrote — Helen McArdell, the Strawberry Blonde, has a repertoire of approximately 2,500 songs committed to memory and sings all by request, averaging 125 songs nightly.

MORRIS: Now, who can duplicate that? I spoke to many doctors and they would say, is there any trick? How can there be a trick, committing all that to memory?

HELEN: I just got mechanical after a while. People would ask for a song and if I didn't know it, I'd go out the next day and learn the song and sing it the next night and that's how I kept adding to my repertoire. I always kept a promise and sang the song the next night if I didn't know it the first night. The only thing that would stump me was if the piano player didn't know the song. I had all I could do to remember my lyrics. I could follow the music and it was easy to put the words to the tune, but some-

times the piano player would not know the music and then that was no good for me.

I got along very well though. Some man used to call up from some place in Texas. He used to come to the Metropole and my piano player, Frank Ross, I don't know where he is now, but he had written a song called "There's No End to My Love for You" and this man liked the song so much that when he went back home to Texas, he'd call up the Metropole and have me sing the song to him over the phone. He liked it so well. But I was very happy there. Morris was the master of ceremonies during that time.

MORRIS: I used to announce—she will present her specialty in a distinctive, unusual manner. When she makes her appearance, she hasn't the slightest idea of what songs she's going to sing until you, the audience, tell her! They couldn't understand it.

Agents would ask me, what song will she open with? I said, I don't know.

HELEN: I worked in places in Jersey where the boss would say to someone, if you can stick her, I'll pay you a drink.

You want to know what kind of life we had. We had such a beautiful life. When we worked, Morris had a grip that he called his kitchen. In this grip he had a percolator, a hotpoint stove, plates, knives and forks, can openers and everything. Now, we would get up in the morning and have coffee in the room. We'd go do our matinee, then we'd cook a steak or something in the room. Then at night we'd have beans and frankfurters and we'd invite all the performers on the bill with us and we'd sit around and talk show business. That to me was really happy days. I enjoyed it very much. I like to think about those pleasant memories.

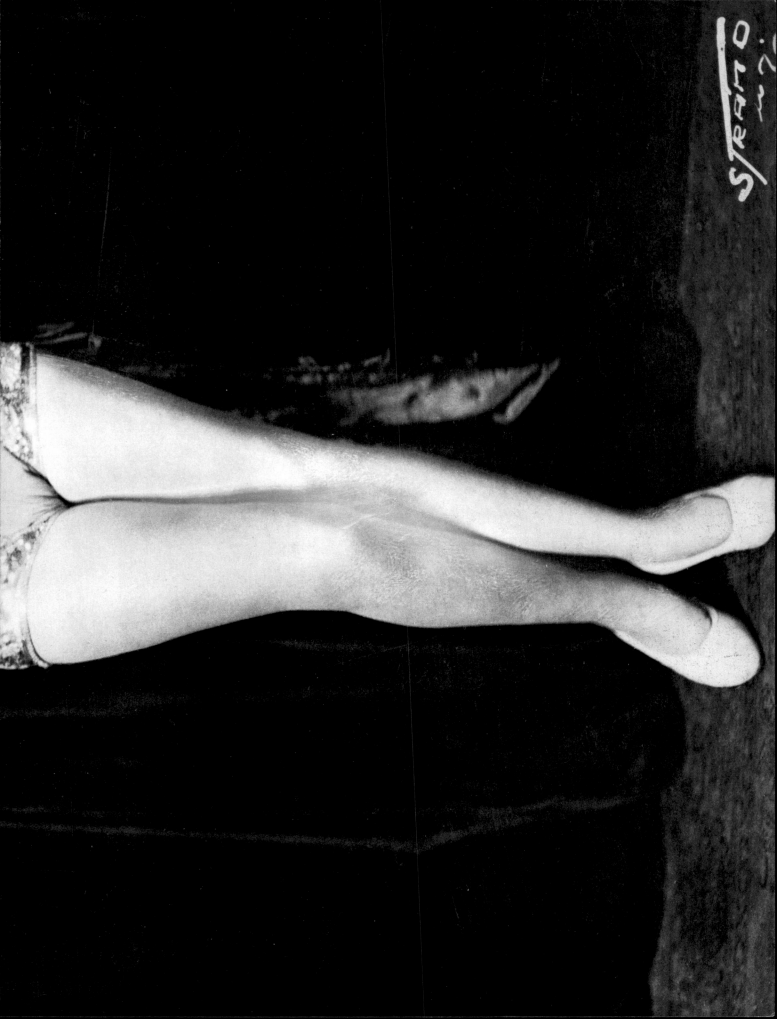

ELAINE STILLER

I went under the name Lynn Lane. My first vaudeville act was in a nightclub in Jersey City at the age of 14. I sang "Alabama Bound" and in those days—this goes right back to about, say, 1930—the men used to throw money on the floor, and I got very embarrassed after the first act and I refused to work.

Then I worked in several other night-clubs like that; I worked all through the country. I met some very fabulous people. Then we worked through cocktail lounges, singing and what have you, traveling all through Europe, meeting all sorts of people. In my day I met Ruby Keeler, although she wouldn't remember. I met her when she was 18 years old. Fred Allen was the most generous, the greatest man who ever lived.

Let me tell you something about Fred Allen. He lived on 58th Street between Sixth and Seventh Avenues. He was such a generous, marvelous man, he used to feel sorry for people who didn't have any money and every night he'd look for these poor men that were probably derelicts and give them money to eat. And one day he couldn't find them, and he couldn't sleep, he worried about it. It's true. Humphrey Bogart was also another man who was very fabulous with tipping, giving money to people who were down on their luck. Georgie Raft, every time he came to New York, he'd go around looking to give money to people he'd known in his lifetime, even people that he didn't know, that he knew they didn't have a square meal.

Those days were fabulous. They had men who'd come backstage and give you flowers or give you diamonds or what have you. Of course, you didn't take them if you were a good girl. That wouldn't be the right thing to do. They'd always try to do what they could to make you their lollipop, you know. In those days, New York was very nice. Very seldom did you have crime or dope. Like people could go to Harlem to Small's Paradise, which was a very nice after-hours club.

During the vaudeville days, I did eight shows a day, traveled all through the country, always on the run, eating in greasy spoons, living in cheap hotels, meeting all sorts of people. One thing about vaudeville —we were all like sisters and brothers, the fellowship was great. Everyone would help everyone. Sometimes you'd meet the circus people and they were the greatest people who ever lived, the circus people.

Now I've turned to picking up, free of charge, in the labor of love, I pick up every homeless animal I can find that doesn't have a home. So I fill myself up with all kinds of dogs and cats, emaciated, starved, and I house them in three apartments. Through donations, I'm able to feed them and I have to go to high-class restaurants at three in the morning and pick extra food from the garbage pails in order to feed them. I adopt cats through free ads. I've had movie stars who have helped me like June Havoc, Gypsy Rose Lee, Kay Francis, Vivien Leigh, who played in *Gone With the Wind,* all these wonderful people are gone except June Havoc, and I don't know where she's moved to. She used to live around the corner from me. Let me tell you what happens. I go through the garbage pails sometimes and I can hear a cry and look, and bang, you find some kittens that were disposed of. How horrible people are. Also with puppies, many puppies I've found that way.

I never thought much about animals, really never knew much about them because my family weren't animal lovers. I came from a very ultra, ultra-beautiful home, where Mother was one of these queen bees who didn't like anyone to dirty her house. Well, I came to Broadway to work in a show here and two little boys were running on Broadway and 45th Street. They had broken the window of a pet shop and stolen a little white kitten, it couldn't have been no more than four weeks old, and the police were running after them. Well, the boys were going to throw it down in front of Bond's Department Store in the sewer and I grabbed this little kitten from them. I didn't know more about kittens than

118

the man in the moon. I was all of 17 years old.

So here I take this little kitten and didn't know what to feed it. I met a woman in the park and she told me to get a bottle. This is how I fed this cat. That was my first love of understanding animals. Then about three weeks later, I saw a cat through my window running across the street and he looked starved. Well, I thought, this is great, the neighbors will have great respect for me, so I brought some food down to feed him. Well, you don't know what happened. I went down to feed it every day for three weeks, and he brought his boy friends and girl friends along with him, and before you knew it, I was evicted from my neighborhood. People are so evil, they don't realize that an animal is a living creation of God just like we are, only they're defenseless. They have no one to fight for them. It's a pitiful thing that they breed, but they do. People adopt animals from shelters, then they get tired of them because they haven't the patience till they're trained and not mess up the house, so they throw them in garbage pails, or on the street to starve for themselves. So this is how I got into this animal work. Before you knew it, I was feeding 300 cats. I've been in newspapers and on television. It got to the point where it became a way of life.

Then I heard about the shelters where they take them and sell them for vivisections; that means useless, suffering research. And other shelters, private organizations, where they don't even investigate people they give animals to. I heard only recently of one man who had seven dogs in one year and they all disappeared.

But people in show business, all in all, are very lovable, although some of them might forget that they were once down in the dumps at one time. But most of them have lovely personalities and are very generous.

STRAWBERRY

I got the name Strawberry traveling in a show years ago when I started performing. Been in vaudeville practically all my life, singing, tap-dancing and telling some jokes. I started at 15 years of age in Ringling Bros. Barnum and Bailey Circus. Left home and went to the circus for about seven years. They used to have side shows then, and I'd tap-dance and sing. They had like vaudeville shows on the side, besides the circus, about 20 shows a day, we'd never stop from morning till night.

Then I went into real vaudeville. Then into shows at the Palace. Went from one show on Broadway to the other. I've always followed the principals of big shows. Somebody had to be the main guy, and I'd always follow or replace someone if they couldn't make it. I was in the Palace for four or five years. I played all over the U.S. on the Keith Circuit. Then I traveled for years with the minstrel shows and played the part of the principal comedian in the show.

I'm 83 years old. I love to entertain people, it's just something that's in me. It makes me happy, I guess, that's why. It's nice. Some people see me and like me in a show, and they ask me to perform at some special function, and that's how I get around.

I never married. Had no time. I was always on the road. I was in London for seven years in theaters and clubs back around 1929. I was also in Paris.

I was born in New Orleans, Louisiana. I've always liked to entertain. It's something that surprises even me. It wakes me up unbeknownst to myself. I do a show and keep trying to improve myself and add to my act, and it keeps me going.

Yes, I've played all over. I worked once with Lena Horne out in Los Angeles. Went out with her, too, but that's all I'll say about that.

I keep myself busy. I made a violin out of a cigar box.

I don't know what to say to young people. I don't know how they feel about living the life I've led. They'd have to want to do it. I'd help anyone anyway I could. I'd tell them to keep up with their music and singing and dancing as long as they're intending to stay with it. I think I had the drive to be a star — that's what keeps me in it. I still want to be a star.

CLARICE WITHERS

I'm Clarice Withers and I'm a senior citizen, old in years, but young in spirit.

Well. How should I start my story? It's been such a long time since I've been — been doing anything at all in show business. When I first started I was only about 15 and went on the road with a musical comedy and traveled one-night stands, one after another, each town one night, and then the show folded and our producer, he just skipped with all the money and left us stranded, but if it wasn't for Equity who sent us the money to come back to New York, we would have had to have — well, we probably would've had to walk home, way out from Marietta, Ohio. Well, we came back to New York and it was just wonderful. Times Square looked so good to me. I love it — I still love it. It's very exciting although it's — even though it's passé — almost passé, with all those big buildings and office after office after office.

In those days when I was a young girl — why, oh, those bright lights, those theaters, one after another. The dressed-up ladies and men — oh, there was such gaiety — seems to me that was — you know — we always like to think that the past was always the best, but there was such a gaiety that's stayed with me all these years. I loved every moment of it.

I did a few shows — oh — I did *Old Heidelberg* and *Student Prince*. Then I worked in the Latin Quarter on 48th Street. It was a nightclub. Dancing, yes. We had individual parts and we each did something. I impersonated Gaby Deslys, she was — oh she was really big at the time and, I being French I suppose, they gave me the part because it suited me. That was in 1921 — way back when. Well, I fell in love, of course, and at the time I didn't have an agent and I had no one to — you know — to give me — to discover me — let's say, although my — the producer of my first show told the crew and the cast that I looked like a million dollars from out front and that someone should get interested in me and, you know, launch me. Well, nobody launched me.

For the next — well, for the next 45 years I did nothing. I stayed home, of course, and my audience was my husband and all the applause I got was from him for whatever I did. Then suddenly my beloved — he just passed away and I found myself completely lost and the first thing I did — was like a homing pigeon — I came right back to the place I love so well.

I landed at the Automat here on Broadway and 46th Street where all the actors and actresses all gather and reminisce about the days of yore and — some of them are still working and doing very well. And I was — well, I was accepted, and then there was a chance for me to do a little work — volunteer work, and when I stepped on the stage — when I got on those boards — oh, baby, was that wonderful! It was just the greatest — it was the thrill of my life. I had been so sad, so brokenhearted, and so demoralized and felt deserted and completely at loss and I had no — life had no meaning whatsoever. It just was impossible for me to go on. Then when I got interested — well, it wasn't that I got interested, just the interest was revived. And I did an adaptation of *Fiddler on the Roof*. And then we did also an adaptation of the Ziegfeld Follies.

So that's it — I'm still at it. Even though I'm doing it gratis. I love it, but of course, naturally, all the marquees are all down, the lights are not bright. It's terrible when you walk up and down Broadway and Times Square and you see all these iron gates up on the windows — it looks like a prison. One cannot stop and look into the windows and see pictures of actors and actresses and — no lights, everything is so dark after 11 o'clock and it's just like a — well, let's say — ghost city. Nothing — nothing, nothing at all. Of course, the kids are today the — well, I don't know what to call them exactly, they're new generation actually but they have sort of a gaiety of their own and I kind of like some of it but — let's say that I still like the Gay Nineties. I'm not — well, I was born in the Gay Nineties. So naturally, I would prefer these days best of all.

Rock music — oh, I love it. I have — I've done the go-go here in St. Mary's and I have a picture of myself doing it and Father

Boyer's sitting in the back on the bench by the piano and he's having the time of his life enjoying it. It's great. I love the beat. I'm just crazy about the beat. Of course, some of it is a little bit too wild and it bothers my imagination. But the lesser tempo — the one — that's — isn't nearly so violent, that's the one I like — I like the best. I like a nice strong beat and I just go all out for it. When I do the go-go I don't sing but when I do sing, I'm every Monday night at St. Mary's. We have a sort of a vaudeville show. Each one does — you know — their bit and their own — let's say — their own thing. We recite, we sing — I sometimes sing a song and then I dance and then sometimes I improvise little songs and I use my own words with it and we have sort of a little skit and we all have a great deal of fun. "Let Me Call You Sweetheart" and "Home on the Range," for instance. What am I going to sing? Last year at St. Francis Church — Senior Citizen Center over on 32nd Street opposite Gimbels — I sang a few songs.

I also sing French songs, of course. We have — when I was a little girl — 12 years old when I was in Paris and went to school there. Of course, once a year we got promoted and all children when the doors were opened wide and everyone of us rushed out and with — you know — glad hearts that it was over and we had all that vacation ahead of us, we had a little song which was very cute.

So that's it. Well, my parents brought me, of course [to America]. But it was a very — my father — well, to begin with, my father had a brother here in America. Well, we were living in Paris and we were — well, poverty-stricken and a very, very poor, very poor and sickly bunch. So when my father's brother sent a ticket to my father and said that you could find gold — you know — that the streets were paved with gold and that

he would — oh, well, he just would become a rich man in no time at all. Well, my father came here and for a year and a half we didn't hear from him at all. We thought he had — we'd lost him or whatever and my mother contacted the ambassador and we found him all right but still there was no money.

It was 1905 and there was a depression and my father had no money, of course, and we were in Paris — very sickly, as I said before, sickly children and my mother got acquainted with Baroness Rothschild through — well, she applied for — you know — subsistence because we were starving and we were — you know — we needed help. My mother put up a fuss and she got arrested and the baroness got interested. And she brought — she liked my mother very well and wanted to open a boutique for her because she made such very beautiful clothes. My mother said that we had a better chance in America than we would have in Paris to grow up and — you know — be useful citizens, so my mother said to the baroness that she was going to take a chance on all the money to — you know — open up a boutique which she lent my mother the money and have — and sent us to America.

So because of the baroness we're here in America and we're American citizens. The United States — is like no place in the world — I — in spite of taxes and holdups of which I was a — you know — what do you call it — a victim, I was held up four years ago and in spite of all that — in spite of the stores all looking like prisons — you know — what do you call it — iron, yes and all that — I don't know exactly how to put it. In spite of everything, give me the United States any day in the week.

Times Square — well, as I said it used to be fabulous. Well, it still is — I don't think it's quite dead yet. There's plenty of excitement still left. For me, Times Square is

→14A   →15   →15A   →16

→19A   →20   →20A   S   M   M

KODAK

→ 16A   → 17   → 17A   → 18

→ 21A   → 22   → 22A   → 23

everything rolled into one. I've traveled all the way out to California and people said there were — you know — very friendly people in California, but I never found them so. I found more friendly people in New York and particularly in Times Square. I've liked everything about it. Even with the crowds and the jams and the pushing and the characters and the drunks and now, of course, unfortunately with the young people who are going on drugs which is so very pathetic, but it to me — it's all together — it's just — I just love it, that's all. I just love, love, love it. All right?

How I met my husband. Well, when I signed up for my first show there was no way — I wasn't getting paid for what I was doing at the time — I mean, during rehearsals we were not getting paid at the time. That was at the very beginning before Equity started and so I had to find some way to make a living and pay my room rent and get something to eat. So at this particular place — say — what they used to call a dime-a-dance hall and I signed for it because I could rehearse during the day and dance during the night. Well, it was 10¢ a dance and we got 4¢ out of the deal and management got 6¢. We danced — oh, to midnight and when the man presented the ten tickets — he usually bought a dollar's worth — and for each dance we got a ticket. Well, I did that for — it seemed for a long time because the show wasn't shaping up very well and we had to rehearse over and over and over again.

Well, this one evening half a dozen sailors marched in and they bought tickets and this man, he looked — oh, well, he must have been imbibing a bit and he leaned up against the wall there and he looked — oh he looked strickly from hunger, he was pale and drawn and half-asleep and I kept looking at him and I came over to him and I said, do you want to dance or don't you?

Well, he said, I don't know how. I said, all right, I'll show you. Well, we danced, and he gave me the tickets, I took all the tickets and then — nothing, nothing happened. Except that he said he was going to one of the islands and would I like to — how would I like to go to Bird of Paradise and I said — oh, all you boys are the same. You promise girls the moon and you just don't give it to them.

Well, later on I didn't see him again because I went with a show on the road and months later I came back to the dime-a-dance again because I was looking for another show. I was between shows and I had — then I had to earn something. And I met his friend and asked about this man that I had danced with and he gave me the telephone number — no, he didn't give me the telephone number. I gave him my telephone number and I met him, he called me and I met him again, met again and inside ten months we got married.

Oh, I wasn't aware of it, of course, but this friend of his said that when he saw me — when this man saw me he turned to his friend and he said, you know — see that little girl there with the blonde curls and the big feet. You know, actually I didn't have big feet but my feet used to be sore from dancing and you know, from dancing with so many of the boys, and there was — sometimes I danced with as many as 750 dances a night. And that was some dancing and I had to get large shoes, naturally, about two or three sizes bigger than my feet. And to him I had big feet. He turned to his friend and said, see that little girl with the curls and the big feet — I'm going to marry her. And we did, ten months later. And we were married for 45 years, till he passed away — the tragedy of my life. It was the tragedy in my life in having lost him, but the blessing was that to me he was just the stars and the moon and the sky, my lover, my mother, my father. My whole family, because I was so very young when he married me.

He was such a gentle soul. He came from out west. He had — well, he was just a darling. Just a wonderful darling. Oh, well, no, he was a sailor when I met him. But he went — after we got married — we went to Chicago and he learned a trade, came back and became a projectionist — motion picture operator, so he was more or less in the industry. He was part of show business. So that's it. It's not very exciting.

No, I don't know of anyone else that had married — well, when I worked there. 'Course, when I first worked at this dime-a-dance place, it wasn't filled with hoodlums and cutthroats — you know — holdup men and Mafias and what have you. It was just a nice clean place. As a matter of fact, when I applied for the job, Mr. Wilson looked at me and says to his partner, take over. His partner's name was Prince, and he said, take over — I'm going to take this little beauty out for a ride in a hansom cab and show her off all over Broadway, Times Square, yes. And we rode — oh, I had a big picture hat and my hair was all in curls and I had golden hair at the time. And I must have been pretty — they all said so. They all said so. How old was I? At that time about 15. It was great.

Growing old gracefully is an art — it's also very hard, because there are so many things to discourage you along the way. You watch the other people in your generation and you wonder why they look like so many vegetables all in a row. You go into some of the senior citizens centers and there they sit, with expressionless faces, and no will to live

and no will to go on. And as far as saying — oh, well, I'm on the way out — what the heck. So it's another couple of years, so what. Life is so uncertain, you could die at any time, from the minute you're born till the minute you're dead — why you die anytime, young, old, middle-aged. It has no specific time for dying. So if you keep your brain working and that in itself is an achievement and a thrill to learn new things no matter how old you are.

One of the things that I — I still have a very hard time trying to learn my songs — I come back again and again and try again and again and make my poor old brain work for me. But it's very discouraging to watch the others not trying. And it makes you so sad, makes me very sad. That's why I like to mingle with different age groups — not just the very old or the very young. I like teenagers and I like people in their 40s and 50s and little children. As long as I live, I want to live — to feel young, even if I don't look young I want to feel young and I feel very young inside of me. And I try to — I try not to think of the end of the road — every once in a while I break down and it makes me — oh, it's — one of the things that makes it so hard to grow old gracefully is when you're alone. If you have a mate, if you have someone beside you — you exchange views — you see a beautiful painting, you say — oh look, dear, isn't this just beautiful, look at that tree, look at the sky, look at the grass, look at the flowers, but I can't say it to myself. I'll turn around sometimes if there's no one there for me to express my joy and delight. I think life can be beautiful at any age, young or old.

JOHNNY GUERRE

Emil John Guerriero is my family name. Johnny Guerre—that was my stage name since 1916 when I went into vaudeville. I was born and raised in Greenwich Village. My father had his business there; my whole family was raised in Greenwich Village, all brought up there. Greenwich Village was one of the finest sections in New York when I was born, in my time.

How did I get into vaudeville? Well, we used to perform with Joe Campo at all weddings that took place in Greenwich Village. I sang and I danced. I was originally a comedian. We were both comedians when we went in. I left high school and went away from home to go into vaudeville, and I thought my parents would be very angry when I came back, when they found out, understand? And so, they missed me. I didn't tell anyone where I was for about three months. They were worried, of course. But everybody in the neighborhood says, no, he was offered a job with The Nine Crazy Kids, the school act.

That was the first act that I was in, at the old Fourteenth Street Theater, 14th Street and Sixth Avenue next to the armory. We roamed. We went and got a room. In those days, we had theatrical boarding houses which were wonderful and very cheap and all you wanted to eat, and a nice place to sleep. I was 17 then. But since I was 15, I was singing at parties and doing Italian comedy and straight. I didn't have to audition. In those days, auditions meant nothing. Today auditions mean a lot. In those days, if you had an act, you'd go up to the agents, tell them what you got, run off a number, sing it, do some of your stuff. Okay, you're booked. And we worked all the circuits in the States.

The first act I was in was called The Nine Crazy Kids. That was a school act — four boys, four girls, and a teacher. It was very good. We had a sissified fellow, we had an Italian comedian, we had a straight man and a rough guy. I was the straight guy 'cause I was the singer. I used to sing "Memories." I had a very fine voice at the time. I don't have that voice today. I sang "Memories" and "Oregon." "Oregon," I sang with an Irish accent. "Memories" was a very important song for me at the time. Everybody used to ask me to sing that. We had an Italian comedy song that we used to sing, and everything went over because in those days, every theater had eight vaudeville acts and a silent picture and the news.

And everything was cheap. That's why families were good. Every man took his wife to the theater, Saturdays, Sundays, holidays, took them to dinner. Dinner was cheap; theater was cheap. Understand? And everybody enjoyed life those days.

But today everything is changed. The churches are changed. The people are changed. Everything, everything is changed. I have seen so much change since 1900, you know, since I was being brought up and I don't like it this way, but one person can't do anything about it. It must be done with the majority of the people, understand? That they can get together and stop this nonsense that's going on. In those days you didn't have to lock your door. You had a little five-cent key that turned the door; you could leave it on top and when the kids came from school, you could take it. Nobody robbed us, nobody hurt us, nobody bothered anybody in those days. Nobody. I never remember anything in my childhood coming up where anybody had trouble. And that was Greenwich Village, and today Greenwich Village is bad.

Today I have my own theater, and this is the cleanest Broadway show in New York. We show no play with anything off-color. That's why we have Oscar Wilde's play with *A Woman of No Importance* and *Lady Windemere's Fan* and the people are just wonderful, the performers. Because that goes on their résumé that they were here and they have a copy of their program and it helps when they go for another job. And none of these people get paid. And we don't even charge; we just have a contribution basket. If they put it in, we accept it. And this is an Equity showcase. I got permission from Equity for producing this show. This is the second one I produced. The others were produced by somebody else.

Now I began producing them myself, see, because it's my theater and I see that everybody's acceptable. We got all nice boys, nice girls, and they're all decent people. Not all are Equity people. We have four or five Equity, and the rest are regulars. But we must get permission from Equity, we got to sign the papers, and we have a deputy who's in charge of the Equity people. He sees that everything is right, that we have the ladies' room, the lighting, and that everything is in order. And he could report us to Equity, that's why we don't do anything wrong. Stagelights Theatrical Club, Inc.—it was formerly a performer's club. We used to call this a performer's paradise when we opened up in the hotel years ago, in 1952 I think. We started before then, but then we went into the hotel, and the rent was being raised. Then we went to 46th Street and they were raising the rent, and then we came here, and we been here over ten years now in this theater.

I have a good director, I have a good star what we call, like a stock company. See, we want to make a stock company out of this. If we can find the people that we pick from this show and the last show, we will keep them and they will work in every show like we used to do when I was in stock years ago. Everybody did all the plays. See, the old stock companies, you have a group, you clean up the place, you help, you work, you build, you build tables and chairs and everything. You also perform. Then you also have worry about the stage lighting, the set and who builds this and who takes care of the program and the flyer that you have to send out. It's a lot of work.

When I look back on my vaudeville days, I remember them as the finest days of my life. They were happy, you had all the friends you want, wonderful girls and wonderful boys. We used to eat together, we roomed together. In those days we'd get a room all through Pennsylvania, 50 cents a night. I've been in places for 35 cents a night. We traveled all over the country. We were on the Loew time, Keith time, Sullivan concert time. We toured all circuits and you were booked and booked and booked. An actor in those days could work 52 weeks a year without getting any time off. Of course, you didn't work hard. You had an 11-minute act, you worked for 11 minutes and you were through. Some theaters, you worked two a day, that was big time, the Keith circuit. Then all these small theaters throughout the country, you worked three and four shows.

The only show I didn't like was the supper show, because everybody went home to eat and most of the people were sleeping so then you eliminated a lot of stuff. See, you just killed time. Nobody liked the supper show, because if you don't have a full audience, you cannot enjoy performing. I found out the other night, we had four people one night when they were checking the rehearsal, you know, rehearsing and checking the mistakes, and they couldn't do so good. Now, the night before last, we had 17 people, 18 people—the performers did a beautiful job, because they saw an audience. And if you see an audience, it's wonderful. It's a thrill. If you come and see the show, you see what I'm talking about. Each one thinks they were on a Broadway show, making $500 a week, $1,000 a week.

In vaudeville, I always had a trio. I worked with a girl, I worked with another fellow, Joe Campo, always with somebody.

When I worked with the trio, I was the manager. That was my act. Ed Reed and George Sylvester, one was from Cleveland and the other from Texas. We did song, dance and comedy. When vaudeville stopped, they had no money to get back where they lived, so they stayed at my mother's house until they got the fare together, the train fare. So my mother used to give them breakfast, I would take them up some lunch.

We used to have in those days McFadden's Penny Restaurants. He had two restaurants, one on Myrtle Avenue, Brooklyn and one at 43rd and Sixth Avenue. He did that for the performers. You'd get beef stew for a nickel, bread and butter, two cents, everything. They both passed away now, but I kept in touch with them up until ten years ago because I wanted to get them back here. See I run a ball every year, dinner, entertainment and dance. I run it at the Beekman Towers, at the Waldorf Astoria. I had my guest of honors, a very good show I ran at the Piccadilly for four years. In September, I'm running at the Starline Inn. But when I contacted the one in Cleveland, I wanted the trio to perform at the dance, I found out he had passed away. Then I contacted the one in Texas, and I found out he was sick, and then he died. So I'm the only one that's alive. I know Ed Reed was in an office, a banking office, after he went back to Texas but what George Sylvester did after vaudeville, I don't know.

In those days when an act broke up, and you went out West, when they went home, that was it. Finished. What are you going to do? I was with them in the same act for four years. Now that's a lot. One time one of them got sick, the other one wanted to lay off, that's when I went with a girl, a partner. We did song and dance. She was a good dancer, tap dance. I did my songs and she tapped. That was her specialty.

Today, when we go to a ball, I don't even dance. My legs, you know, and my age. I'm going to be 74. I'm in good condition, thank God. I never smoked in my life, never drank in my life. Never. And I always had breakfast, good lunch and a nice dinner. And in vaudeville days, you take a girl to dinner, a dollar, both of you eat. If you left a quarter tip, it was beautiful. If you left 25 cents tip, the waiter was happy. I remember Rosoff's on 34th Street, we used to go to Rosoff's. A lunch — 20, 30 and 40 cents for lunch. You wouldn't believe it, would you? Ask the manager there, he'll tell you.

You know, vaudeville will never come back. You will never have the days that we had in vaudeville. Every vaudevillian, before he died, all he thought of was the vaudeville days. I saw actors dying and went to their wake, and on their dying beds, they'd talk about their vaudeville days. Because we were happy. There was no such thing as robbing an actor. All you gave your agent was ten percent, and you were booked. All expenses were paid, train fare and all, which was nice. We used to sit at 38th Street and Eighth Avenue. The meals they would give us on a Sunday and we'd sit and talk about this act and that act.

And I remember when George M. Cohan was president of the National Vaudeville Artists, he liked me and we used to sit there; he gave me a tie, I still have the tie, made to order on Fifth Avenue. He said, that's your parade tie — anytime you're in a parade, you put that tie on. And I still have it, I never wear it, but I still have it in my closet. I keep it for my collection.

I have a collection, you know. I had a display at the Union Square Savings Bank for six weeks, all my stuff was in a showcase. And I got a letter from John Golden who's a big man in the theater, and I sold him a milk can engraved — the 500th performance of *The Dairymaid* — and it was a milk can they gave out. And I saved it for myself and I sold one. He wanted it, and I would've given it to him for nothing, but I got myself $100. But I think he promised this woman that he would try and get it because that woman went to that show and she asked him about it. I told him, Mr. Golden, you're a wonderful man in the theater; you can have it. I'm known for that. I'm on the board of the Catholic Actors Guild, too, you know. I'm a life member of the Catholic Actors Guild. I used to work with the man who died, Walter Winchell. We used to sell the *Vaudeville News* for five cents on the corner of 46th and Broadway. And I've been looking for a *Vaudeville News*. I had them but they were destroyed in the moving, and getting married, and you don't find these things anymore. I wish I had all these things that I actually wanted.

I never was booked into the Palace. See, I believe in the truth. I could've played the Palace with a girl, but that time I was with someone who didn't want me to be with that girl. My present wife, I got a wonderful wife, 31 years, a wonderful girl, good homekeeper, good cook, and good to everybody. She's also a member of the Catholic Actors Guild, and I brought her into the National Vaudeville Artists, I brought her into the Professional Entertainers of New York. She goes every place I go. But she wasn't a vaudevillian. But she goes along with me knowing I love it. You know, everytime, on television when they bring out the old-time vaudeville shows, you ever watch them; I have tears in my eyes. And I'm not going to tell my wife why. I can't tell her why. Because you think of the happy days you had, and then I close my eyes and think of this team and that team, this boy and this girl, what we used to do and every moment was happy in vaudeville

days. I know Morris Lloyd. He used to be good in his day. And his wife, Helen McArdell, was at the Metropole, 10 or 15 years. She was in Ripley's book. A thousand songs from memory.

I get a tear in my eye, though, when I think of the past performers. Most of them are dead, now. I ran a ball at the Waldorf Astoria and then we had a dance, and I was sitting and a guy looks at me and it was Joe Smith of Smith and Dale. Charlie Dale died. And Joe Smith looks at me and he says, you're a performer. I says, that's right — you were my guest of honor, you and Charlie Dale, at the Waldorf Astoria. I used to have all the big ones at my ball. That was back about ten years ago.

My song "Memories" went like this:

Memories, memories
Of the days gone by.
Along the sea of memories
I'm drifting back to you.
Wildwood days, childhood days
Among the birds and bees,
You left me alone
But still you're my own
In my beautiful memories.

The Irish song I sang with an Irish accent went like this:

Oh, Pat McCarty in Arty living in Oregon
He heard a lot of talk about this great New York.
So he left the farm where all was calm
And he landed on old Broadway
He courted little Mary and into a swell café
When the waiter brought the cart to Pat
And said, what will you have,
Why, Pat looked at the prices
And said, huh, I'll have me hat.
I'll go on, I'm gonna go back to Oregon

I'll go on, I'm gonna go back to stay.
You know, I could buy the houses and
   many a bale of hay
For all that I got to pay to feed a chicken
   on old Broadway.

During the First World War, I was on
the USO circuit. I knew Lillian Ashton, I
knew her for years, she's an old-timer. I
have an NVA book — in there you can see
real vaudeville names. Nobody has a book
like that.

See, when we worked in the theaters, we
also had to do benefits, no pay. Then we
had what you call private. Like in York,
Pennsylvania, a very wealthy woman came
to the stage door and said she wanted that
fellow in the middle of the trio, which was
me. So the stage door man said, "Johnny,
there's a lady in there wants to see you."
We were called the Lime Trio. Then I had
the Johnny Guerre Trio. See, we changed
for different bookings. An agent would book
you under a different name in the same
place and the owner of that club or theater
won't know that. So, anyway, this lady was
giving a party and she wanted two or three
acts and she would pay well. She would
pay in one night what we made all week.

Once I was called out again in Tuxedo
Park, a very wealthy neighborhood up in
Westchester. We did a show up there, spent
a weekend there. They even did our laun-
dry overnight. We got up and we couldn't
find our underwear. Couldn't find our shirts
or anything. The maid came to our door
around 8 o'clock to call us for breakfast and
we said, where's our stuff? She says, oh,
they're all washed, they're in the dryer in
the cellar. They had gas dryers in those
days.

I worked with them all. Everybody who's
big today was on the bill. Take Georgie
Jessel. Take Al Jolson. Al Jolson never
played the Palace. He went from vaudeville

— he had a brother, Harry Jolson, who was
a blackface comedian, and he didn't like
that. He didn't want that because he was
better than Al Jolson. But Al Jolson was
pushed by certain people and that's how
he came about. Al Jolson was sometimes
very peculiar. He wanted for Al, he looked
out for Al Jolson, and that's it. And we
never had too much to do with him, but
when he was in the Winter Garden, we
went to see him in *Sinbad* because we liked
the way he did it. We liked him as a performer because he was wonderful. As a
person I never had too much to do with
him. If I saw him, I'd say, hi, Al. That's all.
He used to mix with the big people — that's
how he got into productions, Broadway productions, and all the big shows. I can't
blame him for that. Listen, maybe I'd do it
too if I was in with them and they got me
into a Broadway show.

Georgie Jessel was very good. He had an
act. We'd have coffee or something. I'd find
my partners up at the Bond Building where
they had the agents, and they weren't
working. So I'd say, what are you doing,
because I'd know them from around. Everybody knew everybody from 47th Street
and Broadway. We used to rehearse at Bry-
ant Hall where the Automat is today. You'd
go in there and get a piano player for 25
cents to run your numbers off. In those
days, you didn't have to rehearse for a
week, two weeks, a month like today. We'd
say, here's my song, and we'd sing, and
that's all. Nothing to it. The girls were wonderful in those days. I had two different girl
partners. For years people used to call me
Broadway Jack because I used to treat
everybody nice. I was in vaudeville from
1916 to the end of 1926. Now I have my
own theater and it's the cleanest off-Broadway show in New York. The people that
we have are all good people. And they like
everything clean.

AL & HARRIET FELDER

I started vaudeville in 1920. I met Harriet in the RKO Coney Island Theater in 1926. I was doing my vaudeville act, Felder and Mann, and she was a terrific dancer in the Big Girl act. Strange as it seems, both acts were closing that weekend. Harriet and I decided to do an act together. It became Ralph Felder and Harriet, and we married a year later. From 1927 to 1937, all that time we worked together, we played all the major circuits, the Orpheum, Loew's, Pantages and RKO theaters. It was a comedy act which we called nonsensical.

Believe it or not, we've been together ever since — 46 years. There comes a time when you have to quit show business and take it easy. We didn't care to travel anymore; we wanted to stay home.

We raised our boy on the road and taught him school until he was 13 and went to high school, and now he is a lawyer in New York. We spent weeks and weeks in national parks, painted deserts, saw some of the interesting spots from coast to coast in the United States. There are no people like show people; you know that song. They are the greatest. Fair and square, a lot of laughs. Worked hard, but had a lot of fun. In vaudeville days, we'd be together for months, we would be together for 40 weeks and we'd become good friends. We went sightseeing and shared experiences in each town. Village Nut Club, Master of Ceremonies 1937–42. When Nut left, he followed Jackie Gleason in the Colonial Inn, New Jersey. He stayed there 16 weeks. I followed him in. It was a tough act to follow, but I lasted 16 weeks also. Now he is a millionaire and I am a happy guy at Showtime Cards Shop. He got married three times and got rid of his wives. The secret of how we get along with each other: we have our little arguments, but we don't make it too big. We have fun together.

You worked steady in vaudeville. There were no layoffs, and you could save a lot. Around 1918, could get $750 a week and everything was less expensive. Sarah Bernhardt got $1,000 a day. She was the highest-paid actress in those days. In those days Sophie Tucker could get $3,000 a week. We did our last show in 1968 — banquets for different organizations. Our car broke down in the middle of the night from Red Wing, Minnesota, to LaSalle, Wisconsin. Rolled down an embankment, rolled over about five times and landed on the wheels. We knew a fellow was coming in about an hour in a broken down Ford. We used our baggage straps to hold the car to the springs and we rolled into LaSalle at 5 a.m. Left our car there. Just took what we needed to do our show. We rented a Whippet car and left our car at the filling station.

The matinee was 2 p.m., and we got there when the second act was on. Harriet had a black eye and I had a bad lump on my head where we hit each other when we rolled over. We put make-up on and made the show. Now, my wife and I left Thursday night after the show, 225 miles to LaSalle to get our car. The Whippet broke down 10 miles from LaSalle, but we saw a car slow up and go faster. See, those guys must be bootleggers who want to see who we are. We flagged them down, but I told Harriet to stay by the Whippet. I said, fellows, my car broke down, can you drive me to town? Hey, fellows, I was in the same racket, bootlegging, but I'm in vaudeville now playing at the Riverside Theater in Milwaukee — help an old bootlegger out. They said, okay, but see what you're sitting on. There were rifles and rum and revolvers and they said, don't get funny. I paid them so they drove us to the Huppmobile people. I took a pillow from my car and had it with me, but I forgot my pillow in the bootleggers' car. Three days later in Milwaukee at the Riverside Theater, the stage manager said, Felder, there is someone out there to see you. We went out there, and there were the two bootleggers with the pillow I left in their car.

That show we did in Miami. I'd say, some show, some night, some night, some moon . . . some bench. And Harriet would say, bench, some grass. Then I would say, some do. And she would say, I don't. We would take each other around from cheek to cheek. There would be a howl. Harriet did a Norwegian accent. She'd say, you have no business dancing while I'm singing. And she would go into a Norwegian speech. Quick chatter. We never did one-liners. We built up. A lot of acts tried it and flopped. I'd say, I like you. There is something about you I like. And Harriet would say, I know, but I'm going to keep it. It all depended on how you said it and the timing. Others tried and it didn't mean a darn thing. All the greats of vaudeville — Jack Benny, George Burns, it's timing that's great. The old performers know the timing. The young performers don't do it daily, so it's harder. I remember when Carson started. Oh, is this awful, but three years he might be good. But now he is great — his timing is sensational.

At this stage of life, we come home from our store. We sit down, have a few highballs, pick up our National Vaudeville Artists Books of the Year and we go page by page. And we remember we worked with them 20 or 30 years ago and wonder what they're doing now. We enjoy remembering, looking at our memories, and those were the happy days. We did our own acts. We would talk together, gags and ad libs. In a week's time, we could do an 18-minute new act. We would condense it. Harriet was known for singing the song — "If I Had My Way, You Would Never Grow Old." Her voice is still good to this day. She did Russian-type dancing tricks. One of the few in show business who did all her dancing in high heels; all marveled at that.

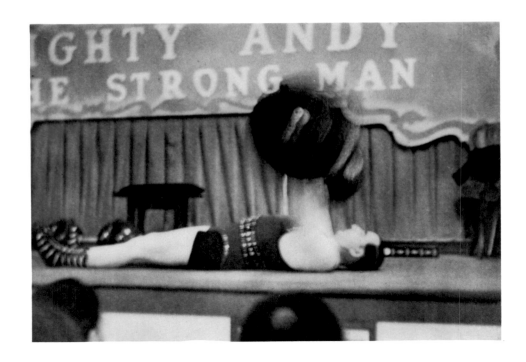

MIGHTY ANDY

I was born on 2888 Fifth Avenue in New York City in 1896. I'm called Mighty Andy, but my real name is Andrew Gioseffi. I was raised in Brooklyn. When I was a child I went to a vaudeville show and when I started, I started lifting cobblestones — you know, the stones they used in the streets here years ago before they had the pavement. Then I used to raise beer kegs they used to have in saloons. I was about 13 years old. I was born strong, though I'm only 5'5½" tall. I'm very muscular. So I went to this vaudeville show, I was interested in lifting. I'm a body builder, too, and I went to this show and saw hand-to-hand bouncers, you know, one man lifts another man by hand. So I got interested.

Then I went home and took off my shirt and went in front of the mirror and noticed I had nice, well-developed muscles. I started to pose like the guy in the show. Then I

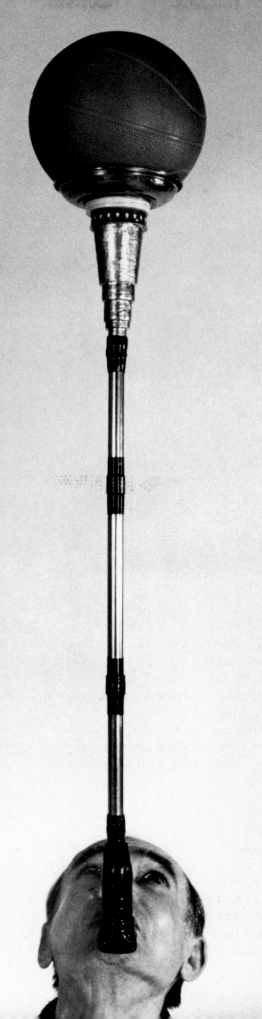

started to lift and lift, and it's a long story. Then I saw a balancing act and I went home and took a broom and balanced it on my chin. You know, everything comes natural to me. The feats of strength that I did all come natural.

So I went to a vaudeville theater one time and I saw a strong-man act. Strongman acts in those days was an attraction. So I went around the stage and waited for this guy and I said, I'd like to be a strong man like you. I was about 15 then. He gave me an address to go to Brown's Gymnasium on 23rd Street in New York City downtown, so I went there and said, I want to be a strong man. The man there said, you can't be no strong man. I says, why not? He said, because it'll cost you $4 a week and you can't afford to pay that, and then he said, you're too short. So I went home and started to lift chairs and this and that, and I developed my own act lifting weights and stuff.

I never belonged to a gymnasium. My gymnasium was my own bedroom, see? Never had any instructions. I still lift, but not as heavy as I used to. Then I started to put on an act and I started to go out and work in shows with my own act. All the feature strength was all done by me, originated by me, and the apparatus was all built by me. Then I used to tear two decks of cards in half. Then I used to take a 60 lb. weight, put it on a pole and support it on the chin and play the mandolin. Or I'd tear a telephone directory in half. And do a two-arm press over my head, 125 pounds, then put it back on my head. Then I used to take a 100-pound weight and raise myself from the floor and move it from hand to hand.

I was going up big and then the vaudeville crashed, around 1929 because of the Depression. Then the sound went on film and the talkies went on film; the radio came up

and that killed vaudeville. See, then there was no more hope. Then radio — there was no television then, radio can't see you, so I used to do little jobs like that, two weeks here, one week there. Then I had a weight 225 pounds, I'd lay down flat on my back and rolled the weight over to my chest and then press it up. Then I had a friend of mine who weighed 215 pounds. When I lifted the weight, he'd sit on the bar and I'd support 440 pounds. I only weighed 135 pounds then. And the muscle pull control is out of this world. No one can control muscles like me. I'm a muscle control artist, too, you know. All this comes natural. Then I broke a 10-inch spike with my chin. The only man in the world that ever did that. I broke all my teeth doing that. It was very hard to do. I used to put, the highest, 200 pounds on my chin.

Then I had to go and work in a factory, working on sewing machines. Things were getting bad, so I figured I'd go to work and build up my social security and get in a union and get my union pension. I didn't do like other performers; they just depended on show business and then they didn't work and they had no social security. I was wise, see? I knew show business would never come back, vaudeville would never come back, I knew that. And the ones in vaudeville that got the biggest breaks were the ones in radio like Jack Benny and Jimmy Durante and all those. They were all vaudevillians at one time.

I had a hard life, but I entertained people. I entertained Fort Dix for five years in New Jersey. I got a medal from the United States Government. I did a lot of work for the Red Cross during World War II, USO, in the camps. I was auxiliary police during the war, I was an air-raid warden. I worked in the factory till I retired but I did shows in between. Like I'd get laid off for one or two months and I'd do shows. Then I'd do shows at night or on weekends. I still do it now. Balancing. I played in a show when Max Baer was world champion fighter, and I played with Fanny Brice in New Jersey. I was on the same bill with her but I didn't know her, I only worked that one day with her.

I never dropped a weight. I even puzzled the doctors when I bent the spike. They wouldn't believe it. A friend of mine used to tell doctors, I got a friend, Mighty Andy, he can break a spike. The doctor says, I don't believe that because a spike could never stand the pressure on the spinal column, it would crack it. So I had to show it to him, and when I did, the doctor told me, he says, Andy, you're going too much against nature. One of these days you're going to fracture a vertebra on your spinal column and be gone, but I didn't care. I wasn't worried. Once I dislocated my jaw doing the spike act; that was the worst thing that ever happened. But I was losing my teeth, so I stopped doing it altogether. Then I had to stop. I only performed in three states, New York, New Jersey and Pennsylvania. I did 10 shows a day sometimes.

I'm a bachelor, never got married. I tried a couple of times, but maybe it was never meant for me.

I met a strong man—his name was Joe Lambert, the world's strongest man, and he worked all over the world, he made a lot of money. I got acquainted with him and we worked together once in a while. He did feature strength, but not like mine—it was different. He did mostly weight lifting. I'm more all around. Recently an agent wanted me to work out West, but I wouldn't go, not now. There's not much money in it, and you'd have to sleep in hotels and travel around. I enjoy myself now. I get two pensions. I'm all alone. If you save too much money, the state will take everything. I

want to take it easy. I'm going to work at the Lighthouse for the Blind at the end of this month, playing my banjo and mandolin, old-time favorite songs and they can sing along with me. They wouldn't be able to see me doing the strong-man act.

I started about five or six years ago to tap-dance. That's another thing I'm gifted with, dancing. I hang around Washington Square Park. They have a lot of bands there, so I dance down there. I used to balance a pole in my ear while I was on the floor. Oh, if you saw the act I do now, you wouldn't believe it. I can sing too, you know. So I put the pole in my ear and I'm on the floor and I start singing. My father didn't like it, he never liked the idea of my working in show business. I wanted to be a doctor once but, you know, in those days there was no high schools, only a few high schools, and they had no money to send me to college. In those days they had to take you out of school and you had to get to work. Things were very hard. Very few boys and girls were graduating from schools. A lot of people in my time didn't know how to read or write. I went up to the eighth grade. Then I bought high school booklets for self-education, you know. But I never got a high school diploma.

I make a lot of people laugh, too, you know. I'm like a comedian. Motions, like. I do a dance in a drunken way in the park, and all the people laugh. I surprise a lot of people, you know. I don't talk a lot about myself, and sometimes I'll be acquainted with people a long time and they don't know who I am. Then all of a sudden I'll do something and they'll say, I never knew you could do that—you never said nothing.

Today is different than it was yesterday. In those days people were more nice to each other, friendlier. You never locked your door because nobody would touch, see, nobody would steal anything. In those days

you could go to sleep on the sidewalk. You can't do that anymore — they'd mug you or kill you. It's like this, if someone comes up to you with a knife today, you've got to be fast and I'd take my hand and bring it up fast and give him a chop in the neck. Then you're all right. But if he gets me first, I can't do nothing. But a person in my trade, it's illegal to hit anyone because I'm an athlete. Like a fighter, a boxer and a strong man, we have a handicap on these people. We know how to handle ourselves. I don't know judo or karate, but I know ways of beating up somebody.

Of course, I've never had to defend myself. But about a year ago, I was doing a show in Brooklyn — Bedford-Stuyvesant — that's a bad place. I was coming home in a subway and I had my mandolin with me, and there were three colored guys there, but I didn't know they were going to do anything. So when the train stopped on Nevins Street, this little fellow grabs my mandolin and he runs out of the car. Now I didn't want to hold the mandolin because they know how to work these things, and the one guy on the end could have taken his foot and jammed it in my stomach or give me a quick blow in the face or something. So I ran after them and I told the people out there — grab him, grab him — but they didn't want to be involved, so we ran upstairs and then he was gone. He must have been doped up or something. That's

the only thing that happened to me. Lucky I didn't get hit. See, I play the banjo and the mandolin while I balance poles on my chin.

I took lessons. I play the harmonica, too. The teacher told me I'd never be a good musician if I play by ear. I had to play by notes. But I stopped taking lessons, bad times and all, couldn't afford to pay, it was 50¢ a lesson, couldn't afford to pay it. I was about 17 years old. I started playing the mandolin when I was 12 for about two months, then I quit because the mandolin wasn't mine and my father couldn't afford to buy one — he was making $10 a week. He was a shoemaker. Rent was $6 a month, three rooms. A ton of coal was $6, and the only ones who could buy a ton of coal were the people making money. We had to buy coal by the pail in the grocery store, 10¢ a pail. Those were some days. We had no steam heat. We had to get up in the morning and crank up the stove. The fire had gone out in the night and the house would be cold. We had just one sink and you had to wash your clothes in one of those galvanized tubs, you know. So how could you go to college? My first job was $3 a week. Only $3 a week. I was working for a jewelry man, he used to sell jewelry home-to-home on time, like 25¢ a week or 50¢ a week to pay for a watch of $20 or something. But that was before I went into show business.

VESTA E. WALLACE

I started dancing school in Pittsburgh
and when I was about 10 years old, I
started to do a single act in vaudeville. I
remember we would all talk about getting
in show business and I would listen to one
and the other and then we'd buy some
music in the 10¢ store and then I'd see people who'd play the theater there in Pittsburgh. Then finally I had this dance I'd
learned in dancing school, but it wasn't toe.
I went in later for toe dancing, and my
mother kept saying, I don't want you doing
this, I don't want you to be on the stage.
But I was so persistent that she just
couldn't stop me. So I got this little act

printed up myself and called it "The Dancing Doll" and I got the letterhead made and she traveled with me. I worked all around the little places in Pittsburgh. I started, I think, at Luna Park, the first place I ever worked. I was too small to go out there alone, and my mother wasn't well, and I don't know how I ever got there, but I managed it. I got $15 for the week which was fantastic.

Once, when I was 14, I did a week at the Harris Theater. I was 14, but I told the man I was 16. I always wanted to be 16, I don't know why, but that was a magic number for me. They put in the newspaper — Miss Vesta Wallace of Pittsburgh is a pretty miss of 16 that gives no odds to many older ones in the profession as a singer and toe dancer at the Harris Theater. That was a little theater that John Harris had that has the ice shows and everything now. I did six shows a day and I was wishing they had eight because I just loved it. I was determined to be a dancer. I can't dance anymore but I can teach. A while back I taught 24 little girls to do a little tap dance like Tommy Atkins, with costumes and all and we put a little show on. I was a good dancer. I did some singing, too, and later some talk.

I was 15 when I came to New York with my mother and we lived on 8th Avenue between 46th and 47th Streets, in a rooming house. My mother was sewing — she was making little rosettes for evening slippers. She had to make 12 of them to get $1. Of course, the lady we were living with thought I should get a job too, so she said to me, why don't you get into the chorus at the Winter Garden? I told her I wouldn't know how and she said to just go and tell them I was a dancer. So, I went and auditioned, and I got in. I stayed for two shows. One starred Al Jolson and the other, Mae West.

Then someone told me that they had people doing specialty work at Churchill's on 49th Street. One night I saw Mr. Churchill and I went up to him and asked if he was Mr. Churchill. He said yes, so I said, I'm Vesta Wallace, I'm a toe dancer. So he looks at me and he says, you are? He looked down at me and said, you come up Saturday night and I'll give you an audition. Well, I said, I don't give auditions. Imagine the nerve of me. I don't know where I got it. So he says, you come up and work Saturday night and if you're good, I'll keep you on. But I knew I was a trained dancer and I wasn't afraid to go, so I said, I'll be up. I went home and told my mother and she made a little dress with a black top and pleated skirt and I went up there by myself to audition and I stayed six weeks. . . .

Later in New York I got in a show. I was in Gia Magison's *Frivolities of '21,* and I had the bathing number where you wore a little short bathing suit and in those days it was kind of risqué. There were two young girls in the show and they did specialty numbers like I did. I thought my legs were too thin and the Barr Twins — they came from Pittsburgh — they said, you're crazy, you got the prettiest legs in the show. I spoke to Irene Delroy, who had big legs, and she said, don't be silly. Anyhow that was the first time I ever thought I had nice looking legs. You know, I thought they were only saying that.

And then from that I did the dancing act and then I met Al Trahan and we worked together.

Al played the piano, but he didn't have much experience as a dancer so I taught him how to dance. He had a lot of ambition. I had him in my dancing act called Vesta Wallace and Co. We worked around for $3 a night apiece because everywhere we worked, they'd say the act wasn't that good. But we kept working and working, and finally we went down to play a Sunday date and I saw Charlie Freeman, a booker that I knew, and asked him to watch our act and tell us if it was good enough to play the Interstate. He said it was good enough and he booked us. . . . It was a comedy act, where I opened as a prima donna and Al was the professor and I'd look to him for the cue. I was very dignified and he was eccentric. He'd fall off the piano stool and get up and twist his stool up higher and then put a piece of paper down to make it still higher and all comedy. I'd sing "Lo, Hear the Gentle Lark" — just enough of it — and when I'd sing too high or something, he'd try to stop me by banging his hands on the piano and when I kept on singing, he'd come out with a shotgun as if he was going to shoot me.

In the second part, I'd come out and do a little rhythm dance in short pants and then I came back out again in another gown and we had a whole talking scene where I was in pictures and he reminded me of my leading man and we went on all through this. I was very dramatic, showing how I'd been in pictures, and he did falls and disarrangements of his clothes. When we got back to New York, we tried to sell it for $500. We had been getting $275 a week on Interstate which was no money. Finally Fox picked us up for $500, then Loew's circuit bought it for $500.

Then we did the Coliseum and Eddie Darling saw us and asked where on earth we had been all this time. We told him we had been playing around the country. Well, he signed us up for three years on the Keith circuit. We were booked at the Palace for one week and ended up staying for three consecutive weeks. We also played six weeks in Europe — London, Glasgow and so forth, and our salary went up and up till it was around, I think, $1,500 a week. And in

1928 it was still going up higher and that's when he got a brainspell or something, thought he was the whole act and said he wouldn't work with me anymore. So that was gratitude.

So I stepped out and he got another girl and he didn't last very long. He finally got sick and couldn't work and finally died. When he was very sick, I felt sorry for him and I went up to see him on 72nd Street, he had to have a nurse come up there and visit him because he had an abscess on his lung and it was open and they had to dress it — oh, it was awful. Then he finally died of cancer of the lungs. . . .

We met lovely people in show business. We were once on a bill going out to the Coast with Lou Cody who was a picture star, and we went out to his house in Hollywood. I met Mabel Normand, who I'd always admired as a child. I knew Fanny Brice and she was a great admirer of mine. She did a little painting and she wanted to paint my legs because she thought I had such beautiful legs. That always struck me funny when people would say that. Once I sat at the table with Fanny in Denver and she asked me if I liked hard-boiled eggs, and I said yes, and she ordered the eggs and fixed them herself with a bowl of onions. So we had onions and eggs which I thought was very interesting for a woman of her caliber. She was a very big star. . . .

When I first went to Europe, I was on a ship with Nelson Eddy and he was going over there to study and we became very friendly. He stayed over with a lady that was sponsoring him to see Europe and show at the Palladium. Then when I would call Nelson here in New York or go to the theater, he made a special effort for me to have a seat even if it was sold out, no matter where he was, his concerts. Once he was over at the Mosque Theater and I was visiting a friend of mine in Newark. I sent my name back and they immediately brought a staff to the front with seats and I spoke to him afterwards.

When people get really big like he did, you can't have too much time to reminisce little things like we could, although I know when he was at the Center Theater and I was listening to him and I thought, gee, that must be the Nelson Eddy I met on the ship, so I went over and sent my name back and he came out to the door. He said he only had a few minutes but he said, I want you to give me your name and I'll call you after the show, so I wrote it on a little piece of paper and he had his evening clothes on and I thought, oh well, I know what success is, he won't call. Well, he did. . . .

I knew Cary Grant very well, too. He was doing an act with a man called Jack Janis and Co. It was two men and a girl and they said, Vesta, if you'll come and work with us, we'll call it Vesta Wallace and Co. I had just split from Trahan then, you see. And his name was Archie Leach and I went up to the Regent Theater at 116th Street, my mother was here and I was going to sail in a couple of days. I went in because they were playing there and I went into the dressing room and said I was sailing in a couple of days. And Archie Leach said to me — gee, Vesta, are you lucky; I'd love to go to England, that's my home. I never forgot that when I saw how he built up. I've never seen him since and I never made any effort to see him. I often think I would just like to see him but, of course,

when a person gets so big — not everybody — but some people like to say, gee, wasn't that great, or something, you know.

George Burns, too, I knew him. He was on the bill, his name was Nat Burns and he did an act with Lorraine. Burns and Lorraine, before he ever worked with Gracie. He said he was going to do an act with a girl and I said, you — with that voice? You can't talk! So there you are. How about that. Fabulous, the success he's had. Well, I'm telling you. Everytime you look, someone wants him on their program. So nobody can tell. I looked very successful when I met him, but he outshadowed me. That's life.

Once I got the Best Dressed Woman of the Week award here in New York by Symes Silverman's wife who owned the *Variety* and in another paper called *The Skirt*. They said I didn't only know how to order clothes, I knew how to wear them. . . .

A man I know says, you're a gorgeous, gorgeous creature. I say, people when they look at me now don't think that I was anything outstanding, but it's nice to hear. Then there's another man who comes in the magic store and he starts — oh, you should have seen Vesta when she was at the Palace — things like that, but, as I say, it's nice. Of course, there's an awful lot of jealousy. When you get older especially. People that had never done anything in their life and you even mention you've been in show business, they're mad, I don't know why. They're jealous, I guess.